IMMIGRANTS

D1270763

Robert Harney and Harold Troper are both professors of History, Dr. Harney at the University of Toronto and Dr. Troper at the Ontario Institute for Studies in Education. Dr. Harney is President of the Multicultural History Society of Ontario.

IMM

A Portrait of the Urban Experience, 1890-1930

Robert F. Harney and Harold Troper

Van Nostrand Reinhold Ltd. Toronto
New York   Cincinnati   London   Melbourne

IGRANTS

The source and acknowledgement of quotations appearing in this book are to be found following the relevant quotations. The sources of photographs are listed at the back of the book, this list being considered for legal purposes to form part of the copyright page.

ISBN cloth 0 442 29948 6

Library of Congress Catalogue Number 75-27151

Design by Brant Cowie/Artplus

Printed and bound in Canada by the Bryant Press Limited

77 78 79 80 81 82 76 5 4 3 2

Canadian Cataloguing in Publication Data

Harney, Robert F., 1939 –
  Immigrants

ISBN 0-442-29949-4 pa.

1. Toronto, Ont. – Foreign population. I. Troper, Harold Martin, 1942 –
      II. Title.

FC3097.9.A1H37 1977	301.45′1′09713541	C77-001293-0
F1059.5.T689A24 1977		

PREFACE

In the 1890s, Clifford Sifton became Minister of the Interior and began the aggressive peopling of Canada. He did so within the framework of the British Empire in which he believed. In those years, the definition of an ideal immigrant for Canada and of a perfect immigration policy was born. Unabashedly colonial, the government defined immigrants not from the British Isles as "foreign." Unembarrassedly North American, they excluded immigrants from the United States from the category. So the ideal immigrants were of British or American stock, were independent farmers, and would settle in the West. Sifton and the government were no more racist in their thinking than the culture of their times. Faced with difficulties in recruiting the ideal settlers, they thought of substitutes in a descending hierarchy, from Scandinavians, Germans and Ukrainians down to those who were, in their minds, less assimilable and less desirable people like Jews, Italians, South Slavs, Greeks, Syrians and Chinese. These latter were the peoples who settled in great number in Toronto at the turn of the century.

Because of Sifton's dream, because of J. S. Woodsworth's skills as a propagandist, and because of the transcontinental railways' importance in national life, the prairies and its port of entry, Winnipeg, became the quintessential centre of the Canadian immigration myth. The North End of Winnipeg was to be the Canadian shibboleth to match the Lower East Side of New York. Toronto, in contrast, was seen as a stable and homogeneous outpost of British society. We believe that the national immigration ideal of that time — self-reliant English-speaking farmers or equally agricultural "men in sheepskin coats" from central Europe—still obscures the reality at the turn of the century. Just as deputy ministers were told in the 1900s to do all in their power to keep out of the country undesirable immigrants from southern and eastern Europe as well as from the Orient and the West Indies, so popular historians have ignored the urban immigrant's place in the nation's growth, or have suggested that such urban newcomers did not exist until after the Second World War.

None the less, it was to the cities that the unwelcome foreign immigrants came. The reason why the government did not welcome them was summed up in the word "foreigner." These newcomers were not English-speaking, not Protestant, not anxious to live in rural isolation, and were, in the lurking racial definitions of the time, "inferior stock."

It was in the city, in Toronto, that the Canadian definition of who should have been the immigrant came face to face with those who were the urban immigrants. It was here that many immigrants encountered the agencies and officials who would try to assimilate and control them. It is these urban immigrants whose story should take its place in Canadian immigrant history alongside the myth of the prairies, the dream of a nation peopled only by Britons or their "racial" equivalent, and the new multicultural myths of the post-Second World War immigrants.

So this is a picture album of immigrant life in a city at the turn of the century. It is also a corrective to the view that "Toronto the Good" was a homogeneous and stable outpost of British society.

The title page carries the names of only two authors but this book could not have been done without the help of many people. Scott James introduced us to the rich photographic resources of the City of Toronto Archives. Every city should have as intelligent a custodian of its pictorial and documentary past. Mary Ann Tylor of the United Church Archives worked above and beyond the call of duty to find the original prints and negatives of photographs that the authors had found only in magazine reproductions. Without a trace of rancour but with a deep sense of the fact that their story was untold in the traditional literature of the city, many families whose parents had arrived in Toronto early in the 1900s actively joined in our search for photographs. Men such as Andrew Gregorovich, Foto Tomev, C.S. Chreston, Joseph Pankowski and Angelo Principe, who have studied and written about particular immigrant communities, gave generously of advice and photographs. Duncan McLaren aided us with information about photographic techniques and his unparallelled knowledge of the ethnic press in Ontario.

Many families and individuals, often the children or grandchildren of the people in our pictures, gave unstintingly of their time. It is they who have made possible the richness of this collection. The authors would like to thank the following: Barry Arbus, the Bernardo family, Daisy Borden, Ann Durjancik, Nan Turner-Egier, John Eisenberg, Joseph Eisenberg, Mr. and Mrs. William Eisenberg, Minnie Friendly, Zlata Godler, Ann Golden, the Henry Goldenberg Family, Mrs. B. Goldman, Esther Grant, Sister M. Joanne (Alfreda Baradziej), the Kujanpaa family, Olga Markovich, Anita Moll, Harriet Parsons, Lillian Petroff and family, Stavros Petrolekas, Morris Roitman, Franc Sturino, the Tatarian family, Helen Tarvainen, the Theodore family, Guy Steacy, Michael Roberts and Trevor Wigney.

These acknowledgements would not be complete without recognizing the contributions of Garry Lovatt, Editorial Director of Van Nostrand Reinhold Ltd., who worked closely with us at every step of production and our editor, Diane Mew, an immigrant herself, who showed patience, good humour, and sensitivity in dealing both with the authors and their manuscript. Finally, we wish to thank our wives, Diana Harney and Eydie Troper, who not only encouraged our effort, but also participated by typing the manuscript, hunting for photographs, and proof-reading.

R.H.
H.T.

CONTENTS

INTRODUCTION

Few of the photographs in this book were taken with the stated intent of depicting immigrants or an ethnic group *per se*. They were taken to record an activity or to point up a problem—a problem, it is true, which often had immigrant dimensions. Still, the Board of Health, the City Roads Department, the Board of Education and various business enterprises had pictures taken for some functional or neutral purpose; the immigrant presence in such photographs, while not entirely incidental, was also not central. The City Engineer, for example, kept photographs of all street and street railway sites and of all buildings being razed. The immigrant in the work gangs may even have been invisible to him. The official from the Health Department photographed premises that were overcrowded or too dirty; he also recorded the visits of nurses to homes, and the noxious back alleys. We do not know how many troubled Canadian households he bypassed to take a picture of the problems of their newly arrived Jewish neighbours. We do not know how much personal hostility he harboured for the newcomer. We know that we have the photograph: we know that if we had chosen to write a volume about poor immigrants from the British Isles we could have found many other photographs in the City Archives that would closely parallel those taken of the foreign immigrants.

The other sort of photograph that is essentially neutral in its purpose is that taken by the immigrants themselves. Such photographs record the rites of passage, such as weddings and funerals. Many portraits were done for transmittal to the old country; outings, picnics, and national political gatherings were photographed to record moments of group concern and happiness. Such photographs were not an attempt to create an ethnic record; they were personal, amateur, and completely unself-conscious. They will ultimately be the richest source for immigrant history, if they can be saved, organized and brought into the public domain, with the proper safeguards for family privacy where it is called for.

A third set of photographs, very important to this study, are those taken in the context of evangelical, educational or social service work. In such photographs, for the most part, the conventions are fairly obvious, and the picture becomes doubly valuable as a comment on the photographers as well as the photographed.

Our pictures illustrate the lives of the new Torontonians: their economic struggles, their efforts to recreate their Old World settings, and their encounters with the guardians of the Canadian receiving society, from the scout masters and evangelists to visiting nurses and policemen. The underlying tension between the immigrant's heightened need to cherish his past, while inserting . himself into the economy and society of Toronto, informs the whole essay. That tension appears in many of the pictures. In the Ward, in Kensington Market, in the Slavic neighbourhoods near the train yards, worlds alien to one another coexisted and sometimes clashed. Our pictures try not to take sides. We do not believe that the immigrant was always the innocent victim of the repressive Victorian ordering of life in Toronto. We do not believe that all the guardians of the Canadian way were nativists or racists. Whatever the balance of guilt, the real historical questions lie in the diffraction of communication and the misunderstanding that existed between the new and old residents of the city.

The dominant society and its authorities fought mightily against cosmopolitanism. They considered themselves guardians of "Toronto the Good," called to defend the city from the onslaught of foreign ways. Such people saw ethnicity as a temporary and pathological state of existence. Macedonians, Ukrainians, Italians, and perhaps Jews and Chinese, once cured of their alien ways, would become good Canadians; so deviation from Canadian norms had to be dealt with patiently but sternly.

The pictures in our album are accompanied by statements made in and about Toronto in the 1900s. We make no claim that the many insensitivities and ethnocentrisms among our quotations were statistically typical of the period. They, like the pictures, exist. The statements were often made by prominent citizens and powerful agents of the society. More appalling, the obvious pathos of immigrant life, as recorded by the camera, seems not to have penetrated the layers of rhetoric and prejudice that dominated the society. So, if the reader, old in the land, shakes his head and says to himself that it was not that way—that his grandfather was "shabbes goy," happily lighting sabbath fires for Jewish neighbours, that the Scottish health nurse was a true friend when whooping cough or scarlet fever struck, that the food inspector received no bribe to approve the family pushcart, and that hundreds of school teachers allowed alien children a breathing space between their parents' values and assimilation—then we ask that reader to thank God for the humanity of face-to-face encounters between strangers who were good people.

Finally, our album has two other simple purposes. We wish to demonstrate the value of the camera and the photograph as historical technique and source. While families discard picture albums of forgotten relatives, and big city newspapers mindlessly clean out old picture files, the tactile and real sense of the city and the immigrant experience fall more and more into the hands of a younger generation of university researchers who measure, compute and speculate about the urban condition at the turn of the century but rarely empathize with the inhabitants. Pictures can redress that failing and rescue the city and the historian from arid statistics about the urban past. The pictures alone, when all is said and done, are sufficient justification for this volume.

1 THE COMING OF THE IMMIGRANTS

Toronto's foreign population had emigrated from many parts of the world. Those who came to Toronto were part of a massive flow to North America that began after 1885. Millions of Jews from eastern Europe and millions of Italians saw their future in the New World. Macedonians, Finns, Syrians, Magyars, Galicians, Poles, Croats, Lithuanians, Slovaks, Greeks and Armenians — all subjects of decrepit yet repressive empires — also came. By the First World War, the cities of the east and the midwest reflected this mass migration of peoples, although the configuration in each city's new population showed the impact of local conditions and opportunities. Toronto, if we use the censuses of 1911 and 1921 as guides, had received its share of the newcomers. By 1911 there were more than three thousand Italian-born in the city and probably about eighteen thousand Jews. There were in addition close-knit and sizable communities of Chinese and Macedonians and lesser concentrations of Syrians, Greeks, Poles, Croats, Ukrainians, and Finns.

An immigrant was a man between worlds; so two places shaped every immigrant experience. The complex reasons why he found himself in such ambiguous circumstances lay in both his country of origin and in Canada. What were the nature of the immigrant's old world setting, his frame of mind and the reasons for undertaking the ocean crossing, and finally the network — commercial or familial — that drew him to Toronto?

Toronto's largest number of newcomers came from the Russian Pale. The Pale was the western area of the Tsarist domain where non-Russians (i.e., Lithuanians, Byelo-Russians, Ukrainians, and Poles dwelt. Large numbers of Jews had lived in the area since the fourteenth century, but by the final quarter of the nineteenth century, life for the Jews was becoming more and more intolerable under Russian rule. New laws in the 1880s forbade Jews to own property outside of towns and cities. Quotas were set on the numbers of Jewish children who could go on to gymnasium (high school). Conscription that meant twenty-five years of military service effectively meant dejudaizing as well. If legislation had become draconian, it was no threat at all when compared with the periodic encouragement that Tsarist authorities gave their Christian minorities to run amuck against the Jews. Pogroms — sudden violent anti-semitic outbursts fed on bloodlust, religious extremism and vodka — destroyed any sense of security that might have developed among Jews in the Pale over the centuries. Although the flow to North America was steady, it was markedly higher in the years im-

1

mediately after a pogrom.

Political and religious persecution was only part of the malaise of the Pale. Jewish immigration had as much economic cause as that of the Italians and Slavs who joined them in the flow to the sea. The Jewish population of the Pale had grown from about a million in 1800 to four million in 1880. Girt about by regulations against owning land or engaging in certain activities, Jews could only hope to expand their economic base in those small trades that they dominated. With the end of serfdom in the 1860s, there had been a steady growth of competition from Christian tradesmen who had the advantage of fellow feeling or anti-semitism to win themselves a peasant clientele. The development of spur railroads also cut into small enterprise. In the *shtetls*, the little Jewish towns of the Pale, Jewish cobblers, tailors, blacksmiths, tanners, hatmakers, carpenters, tinsmiths, harnessmakers, butchers, bakers, watchmakers, jewellers and furriers had two alternatives. They could fall into the factory proletariat that was growing up in the larger cities of the Pale such as Lodz, Vilna, Grodno and Minsk, or they could seek escape. Pogroms, diffuse prejudice, and the threat of mass conscription such as at the time of the Russo-Japanese War in 1905 suggested the latter alternative.

The Italians who came to Toronto might not have been able to recite the litany of oppression that the Jews could, but they too could complain of conditions at home: as southerners, of their treatment by a central government dominated by northerners, as country people (*contadini*), of the selfish exploitation of the countryside by cities, and as peasants, of being treated as *bestie* (beasts of burden) by landlords and by the middle classes of the little agrotowns. No matter how isolated one's *paese*, no matter how limited one's education, there was a political edge to the Italian emigration as well. Most men knew that Garibaldi, the great leader of the Risorgimento, had himself been a humble immigrant, first in Uruguay and then in New York. All could share the sentiment of those farm labourers who had lined up their *zappe* (hoes) against the club of the gentry in a small village in Sicily with a note pinned to them which read, "Pray gentlemen, please till your own fields. We are following Garibaldi to the New World."

The Italians in Toronto came mainly from Calabria, Sicily, Abruzzi and Lazio. There were some immigrants from the Veneto (Verona and Venice areas) and Friuli as well. Whether in the extreme south or the extreme northeast, such Italian areas of emigration had faced rapid demographic change and over-division of the arable land. Many people sensed the need to move on or be destroyed by grinding poverty. Through the port of Naples and through depots like Chiasso and Ventimiglia on the Swiss and French borders, Italians wended their way toward America. The large percentage of returning migrants and the high rate of remittances helped to transform parts of the Italian countryside. In the process, towns and villages became dependent on cash from America and a system of chain migration was born that became its own cause for migration.

Perhaps here we should pause and look more closely at the process of migration itself. North American observers had long oversimplified the causes of immigration. Most Canadians, whether they approved of newcomers or not, saw the immigrant's desire to come here as the logical outcome of a simple set of push and pull factors. After all, they reasoned, in Europe there was oppression, economic misery and overpopulation, while in Canada there was freedom, employment opportunities and rich available land. Such a view of the arriving migrant assumed that all the newcomers wished to become permanent settlers — that they were peasants who dreamed of their own farms on the prairies, or were the victims of political and religious persecution seeking the protection of the British crown. Before the 1900s, the Canadian experience seemed to confirm this view of migration and the immigrant's motives. There had been the headlong flight to Canada of starving and febrile Irish in the 1840s and the planned and orderly resettlement of societies as various as those of the Scottish Highlanders, Galician villagers and the German dissidents of the Russian Empire. The arrival of masses of men from southern and eastern Europe was seen in this same light at first. The Jews of the Pale were obviously fleeing Tsarist oppression and conscription laws just as the Mennonites and Hutterites had. The Italians and Macedonians, Poles and others were the "new Irish"— peasants fleeing headlong from poverty and degradation, leaving behind deserted and devastated villages. (It was no surprise that a high percentage did not become farmers; the Irish before them had become an urban work force.)

Folkloric accounts of the earlier emigrant's plight — oxcarts rolling across Europe, fetid and frail sailing ships, Grosse Isle and the plague: the entire *via dolorosa* of the nineteenth-century immigrant — provided a hopelessly inadequate and antique model for what was happening at the turn of the century. The new migration was massive, a commerce of migration for many exploiters. A good percentage of the newcomers had, at the outset, no desire to settle permanently. Italians, Macedonians, Chinese particularly thought of themselves as sojourners; they sent money from Toronto to foment rebellions in their homeland or to plant a fig tree on a little piece of land they would inherit; they worked twenty years in a laundry or a restaurant and still described their stay in Toronto as an interlude. Like a spurned lover, the Canadian host society despised them for their frame of mind.

Broadly speaking, then, there were two kinds of newcomers to Canada: those who saw themselves as immigrants and those who were migrants, not uprooted but deeply committed to their home village, their family, and

to finding cash in the new world to improve their situation at home. Many, even most, of the migrants, after numerous excursions between Canada and their homeland, became immigrants. Immigration statistics, particularly in a land with "undefended borders," are notoriously inaccurate, but they offer some guide to the frame of mind of newcomers. For example, in 1907 about 4,500 Italian men legally entered Canada (half as many again may have simply walked in from points in the United States). They were accompanied by only about 400 women. The Jewish immigration of that year was 2,000 men, and 1,600 women and 1,900 children. The latter was the resettlement of families; the former suggests the migration of workers. Although it is difficult to count the Macedonians because they fell under Greece, Bulgaria and Turkey in the census statistics, the imbalance between males and females suggested migration patterns among them also. (The rapid growth of political difficulties in Macedonia led migrants to send for families and to give up the idea of immediate return, particularly after the Ilinden rising of 1903.) Toronto had over 1,000 Chinese men and less than 30 women; no matter how long they resided in Toronto, such men must have felt like sojourners.

To begin with, it is important to note that village and town life in eastern and southern Europe and even in Kwangtung Province, China, was not primitive, not isolated or independent from the larger economy and the revolution of rising expectations. Everywhere cash had eroded feudalism and everywhere peasants and small tradesmen could observe those individuals and families who had risen in social status and those who had declined. There was nothing glacial about their social structure; a character in a Sicilian novel commented that "property does not belong to those who have got it but to those who know how to acquire it." Aware simultaneously of the growing amenities in the larger society and of the decline of well-being in the village or agrotown, men were caught between their actual levels of living and their standards of living. Increasing family size and the need to maintain status for all children meant that no family enterprise, whether a Jewish-owned inn or a small Italian farm, could survive without expansion. Families had to run in order to stand still. Periodic disaster in the form of a hailstorm or the building of a railway that by-passed a village inn could destroy the delicate balance and create new immigrants. But even without such a disaster, migration, if not immigration, was necessary. First local seasonal migration, then overseas migration, and finally permanent settlement away from home (emigration) were acquired traditions by which villages and towns tried to avoid the total dislocation born of overpopulation, the collapse of certain occupations and the impact of the money economy.

Almost invariably, the foreground image, the semi-romantic picture of the naive peasant or townsmen leaving his self-contained world of agriculture and ascribed status, breaking the cake of custom to cross the sea to modernity, collapses when the picture is examined in any detail. Of the people who came to the New World city, most left prior trails of migration. For example, Macedonian peasants from remote regions of Kosturke and Lerin had, for many years, sojourned from February to October in the fertile areas of Thessaly or Bulgaria to work with the currant crop or grain crops; tradesmen from the same villages went in the summer as building tradesmen or tinkers throughout Bulgaria. The village depended on this external source of work and cash. A Macedonian village account put it simply: "Those more daring went to work in far off countries. The most courageous decided to try their luck and came to America." Farmers from the Abruzzi went in early spring to work as day labourers on larger estates (*latifundia*) on the Apulian plain. The climatic change because of the difference in altitude between the two areas enabled men to return to sow their own humbler crops after the seeds of the valley were in the ground. Northern Italians travelled into France or Austria as harvest hands or artisans. Many referred to this practice as they would later refer to going as navvies to Canada as going on "campagne," military campaigns. Some farm workers, the so-called *golondrine* (swallows), commuted in an endless summer from Piedmont and Liguria to Argentina. As soon as the Italian harvest was over, they left under sail to plant the crops in the South American springtime.

Young Jews moved about the Pale as craftsmen, teachers and peddlers, but the *shtetls* were overcrowded. The possibilities of new trades or creating new commercial establishments were limited, so the pattern of migration got larger and larger so that men broke from seasonal orbit to shoot out into the larger oceanic adventure. The tradition that brought young men from the crowded villages of Kwangtung to seek work as street hawkers and coolies in the great port in Canton, would by tortuous circumstances carry them from that harbour across the Canadian prairies to Toronto. Despite the flow, migration was only a short-term solution. The rapid population growth and the tendency to distribute the land among all of one's children led to the creation of *minifundia*—farms too small to be productive. Sooner or later, hoe culture replaced plough culture; some children inevitably were denied any patrimony.

While rising expectations, demography, *miseria*, and ethno-religious persecution provided the push factors, available work — the hunger of labour-intensive North American businesses—provided the basic pull factor. Yet none of this was possible without a system, a commerce of migration. The steamship companies and the varieties of agents involved in the migration process were not incidental to the mass movements of people; they were central to it. At first, they brought together the mutual needs of the job-seeking and those in North America who wanted cheap labour. In the end, the commerce of migration itself, in conjunction with the development of chain migration through kinship and village ties, became not the conduit of immigrants but the recruiter. One steamship company, Inman Lines, admitted to having more than thirty-five hundred sub-agents in Europe. Canadian Pacific's agents, through Beaver Lines and sham Swiss colonization companies, recruited illegally throughout Italy. The callousness of the *senseria*, the bounty system used by agents of the steamship companies in Europe, was matched by that of the Dominion Coal hiring agent who told a Royal Commission in 1904 that he paid sub-agents twenty-five cents a head for rounding up Italian navvies.

The trade of the steamship lines and the *negriere* (slave-trader) intertwined with the development of migration and sometimes immigration through family chains. The most remote shtetl in eastern Europe received letters from cities in the New World like Toronto. If the Tsarist censor let the mail pass, there might be a prepaid ticket from Canada in the letter. High in the mountains of the Abruzzi, a young man received mail from an uncle in New York or Montreal or Toronto and dreamed dreams of living in a new style. The hyperbole and the good cheer of such letters, some probably written in the mud of sewer excavations, was born of the warmth of family feeling more than of reality. But there was money, too; it is estimated that over 80 per cent of the savings of the migrants was sent back to Italy, Macedonia and Croatia.

In 1900, an immigrant could get passage to Halifax for about $20; he or she could reach Buffalo or Toronto through New York City for about $25. These, of course, are superficial statistics and a minimal statement of the costs of emigration. Steerage and food costs on shipboard, the seasickness of peasants and shopkeepers on their first ocean voyage, were horrible but predictable, for most immigrants knew what to expect on shipboard from returnees and from the lore of prior immigrants. The real pitfalls, the unexpected and escalating costs came from having to deal with governments, agents and hustlers. One could lose more money getting from Minsk to Liverpool, or even waiting in a harbour inn at Naples, than was spent on tickets for the entire voyage. At the other end, the first *paesano* or *landsmann* who offered aid at the dock in Halifax or New York could be a scoundrel or a runner for ruthless contractors and innkeepers. So it was reaching shipboard in the European port and getting to a destination in the New World that were truly fraught with peril and surprises. Perhaps that is why a city like Toronto often contained immigrants who had intended to settle somewhere else.

The journey began with the decision to emigrate, and there were expenses before one set foot outside the village or town. Although treated like pariahs by their governments, the members of an ethnic or religious minority or the peasants who wished to migrate suddenly found that the government was indeed interested in them. There was something about humble folks packing up and leaving that smacked of anarchy to monarchist officials in central and southern Europe. In the eastern empires people were subjects not citizens. Didn't the flight of subjects impoverish the monarchy? It certainly threatened the cheap labour force of the gentry.

Through a maze of taxes, passports, papers to prove that one was not subject to conscription or that one was not leaving behind indigent relatives, the peasant or the Jewish artisan went cash in hand, trying to buy his way from bondage. If he found too much hostility or difficulty, he could move outside of the legal structures to the agents, brokers, loansharks who could help him leave clandestinely for the New World. By the turn of the century, such brokers were everywhere, and they were often the town notables, not just shady characters. For immigration was a great free enterprise commerce and the commodity was human flesh. For those who had to cross overland to Bremen, Le Havre, or even Liverpool, the dangers were greater than leaving legally and, perhaps more expensively, from a port in one's native land. The competition among steamship lines was fierce; German, British, French and Canadian lines competed for trade throughout most of Europe while the powerful Italian General Navigation Company tried to fight off competition in Italy. Government regulation had improved, and so steerage passengers received a modicum of protection; but hundreds of people were still packed in holds like cattle, fed inferior food and denied access to air and health on the upper decks of elegant and roomy steamers.

For the thousands of Italians, Jews and Slavs who travelled in steerage to New York, Halifax or other Canadian ports, the last obstacle was the most frightening. An eye infection, a heavy cold, an official document out of place could mean detention, deportation, the loss of many generations' savings that had been converted to a ticket. Then suddenly, the regulation and control ended. Some had been ticketed through to Toronto; many others would get there after a series of accidents or misadventures, working along the railway or in other towns. The process of migration or immigration went on in a different way for every man. It had not ended in Halifax; migrant workers might come and go across the ocean many times. If one sees the trek they undertook as a journey of the mind and not just of space, as a search for a better way to live, then, for many it did not end when they settled in the immigrant receiving areas of Toronto.

By purchasing the land from Husein Efendi, the area north of our village increased. However, the problem of making a livelihood was not solved. We were short of many commodities. This forced the villagers to seek employment outside the village. Those more daring went to work in far off countries. The most courageous decided to try their luck and came to America. During 1902 the first men from Zhelevo to cross the ocean to America were Lambro Nikolovsky and Andrea Nikolovsky. With them were several men from the village of Bouf. The brothers Dimitar and Christo Hadji Pavlov, Spiro Dodev and Krsto Dibranov of Zhelevo emigrated to Toronto Canada.

Foto Tomev, *Short History of Zhelevo Village Macedonia* (The Zhelevo Brotherhood in Toronto, 1971), p.75.

The similarity between the conditions that caused many from so many parts of Europe to come to North America is striking. It reflects a complex and almost universal crisis of village life in rural Europe. South Italians, Poles, Galicians, Croats, Macedonians, all found that there was more and more need for cash, more and more need to range farther from home in search of cash. The steamship agents, the tales of pioneer migrants, and continuously rising expectations conspired to turn seasonal orbits into a flow toward North America. The men who went came to be called by national labels in the countries that received them. Canadian officials called them Italians, Jews, Turkish subjects, Bulgarians, Austrians, and so on. Some had a sense of nation, but most were first and foremost village men. They came from Zhelevo in Macedonia, Pisticci in Italy, Bialystok or some smaller town in the Pale; they intended to go home to those towns or to send for people in those towns. Their context was familial, local, "ethnic" but rarely national or statist.

States had tried to impede their migration, and even though they had travelled thousands of miles, they often continued to measure home in terms of a half-dozen miles and familiar landmarks. In a way, the whole process of migration was an attempt by unpoliticized and humble people to bypass states and nations in order to survive.

Below: Macedonian villagers preparing to emigrate, 1923

Right: House-raising in a *shtetl* in the Pale, 1910

A letter from America—envelope quickly torn, a bulky package of papers drawn out, and the family group listens attentively to the news. What! We are going to America at last! At last, we are bound for the Land of Gold, where you pick money up in the streets; where lots and lots of candies are piled up in the schools. These fanciful tales had been often uttered by the town folks, and to our childish ears it was only a few tit-bits of the many wonderful things which existed in America.

Michael Sansone, "Bound for the Land of Gold," in *Ward Graphic* (Central Neighbourhood House, 1919).

Michael Sansone wrote an account of how he got to Toronto from his native Italy. It was written in Toronto for a Toronto audience but he used the generic term America. Sansone had not psychically immigrated to Toronto, or to Canada, or to the United States but rather to *America*, a place and a myth. Italian schoolbooks showed pictures of Columbus discovering America, pictures of Garibaldi as a freedom-fighter in Uruguary and Argentina, perhaps they even had pictures of the Venetian Cabot discovering Canada's east coast. They were all part of a whole, and for unsophisticated small-town people that was enough. Provincial borders, even national borders, did not faze people who had crossed an ocean in search of relatives or fellow townsmen. Men arrived at a certain port because they had managed to take passage on a certain steamship line that plied back and forth between that port and their port of egress. Neither the port of embarkation or the port of entry offers any guide to the immigrant's intended destination or the tricks that fate might play on him. Often U.S. officials would not let people who had passed into Canada from Buffalo or New York return to the United States. The Royal Commission to Inquire into the

Immigration of Italian Labourers (1904) contained an interesting exchange. "Q. How is it about foreigners coming into this country from the United States? A. Well, we do not keep a record of them. It is an open secret that there is some arrangement whereby the steamships plying at ports in the United States get the United States officials to allow these people to pass through to Canada . . . ."

Below: Macedonian girl posing with her parents before leaving for Canada, 1921

Right: Jewish restaurant in Kishinev, Russia, just before the family emigrated to Canada, c. 1923

At the Liverpool Assizes recently, Max Block and Marcus Helfman were found guilty of the charge of defrauding emigrants, and were sentenced to six months imprisonment with hard labour.

They were charged with having "unlawfully obtained by false pretenses and conspiracy the passages of certain emigrants from Liverpool to Canada, by means of ships belonging to the Canadian Pacific Railway, with intent to defraud at Liverpool, on or about the 15th July, 1907, and other days." Mr. Justice Bray, in summing up, said the evidence showed that Block had sent six persons to Liverpool, where they were taken aboard the steamer without tickets, and concealed on board until they reached Quebec. At that port three of the immigrants were found to be disqualified physically for admission to Canada, and they were sent back to Liverpool and imprisoned for stowing away.

The Labour Gazette (Ottawa, Jan. 1908) p.874.

For many of the people coming from central and eastern Europe, particularly the Jews, Liverpool was as important a port of egress as Bremen or Hamburg. In fact, for many Jews, immigration was a process of dodging authorities and surviving. This was particularly true after the failed Russian revolution of 1905. Because of political activities, failure to appear for conscription, or just general difficulty in dealing with the Gentile authorities, Jews often lacked papers necessary to get to Canada. In England, they could find help from Jewish colonization societies and other sympathetic co-religionists. They could recover from the hazards and wear of the trip across the Continent. In Whitechapel in London there was a Poor Jews Temporary Shelter. In the early 1900s an average of five hundred Russian, Polish and Roumanian Jews arrived there weekly from ports like Rotterdam. Some had to stay in London and work in order to build the cash necessary to continue their journey to Canada. Others had to recover their health before they faced the medical officer at Halifax or Montreal. Some, like emigrants from every ethnic group, made the mistake of trusting all people of their "own kind" simply because they were their own kind. The lessons learned about the larger world that way were often very cruel.

Below: Greek Macedonian passport issued to a woman to join her husband in Canada, 1921

Right: On the way to the new world

14

The average steerage passenger is not envious. His position is part of his lot in life; the ship is just like Russia, Austria, Poland, or Italy. The cabin passengers are the lords and ladies, the sailors and officers are the police and the army, while the captain is the king or czar.

E. Steiner, *On The Trail of the Immigrant* (New York, 1906), p.41.

Of the more than five thousand Italian immigrants who entered Canada during nine months of 1906—1907, only seventeen did not travel in steerage. Similar statistics would apply to the other major immigrant groups. Steerage conditions had improved over the days of sailing ships. The Italian government, for example, had stringent regulations that applied to all ships that touched at Italian ports or carried Italian immigrants. Those regulations improved the sanitary conditions and the food service but did little about overcrowding and the class structure that kept those suffering from seasickness away from the clean air of the upper decks. For those who travelled on smaller German and Canadian vessels or left from English ports, there was some protection, but the passenger trade was a business that was attractive to the shipowners only to the extent that it provided high profits. High profits were achieved by overpacking steerage and being niggardly with services. It was not racism and hostility that made the ocean trip what it was; it was simply a matter of calculated free enterprise.

Over two-thirds of the Italians entering Canada in the years from 1900 to 1915 came through American ports. Many Jews came through Ellis Island instead of St. John's, Halifax, or Montreal. On ferries, boat trains, and passenger trains, they worked their way to interior cities like Toronto. In a free society, without the language skills neces-

sary to cope, assuming that uniformed officials that they encountered would be as aloof or hostile as those in the Old Country, the immigrant continued his trek. He had reached Canada without ending his journey and perhaps without sensing that he had escaped oppression.

Right: Italian immigrants en route to Ontario for work

Below: East European immigrant at port of entry

You are already aware that our firm has had your address for several years, having during that time sent you a great number of labourers. They received from you all the help and information possible regarding work and we have no doubt that our sending you such men has caused you some trouble.

You are also aware that our firm is corresponding with the Societa Anonima di Emigrazione della Svizzera as well as with other agencies of emigration of Switzerland which have been regularly and legally constituted. You do not ignore that a brother of Mr. Schenker, one of those who has opened an office in Montreal for the exchange of money in order to compete with you has lately opened an office in Chiasso, Switzerland and got passengers from Italy through the help of Schenker who is in Montreal. The latter sends to his brother in Chiasso notices and orders for the shipment of men and his brother reads the notices to the passengers, mentioning the ships they ought to go by.

Having had knowledge of this action on the part of Schenker we took the liberty of addressing ourselves to you in order to advise you and inform you thereof and to ask if it would be possible for you to do something for us in the matter.

In order to facilitate the thing for those who wish to go to Montreal through friends you can exact yourself in Montreal the amount of the passage money. Send us an order for shipment saying at the same time that you should pay us only 170 francs from Chiasso to Quebec. All that you can get above that from the interested parties will remain to your benefit.

It is understood that our shipments will be executed as far as we are concerned with accuracy and precision. We enclose herewith a list of the dates of sailings of the ships of the CPR plying from Antwerp, and we beg you to reply to us and hope that the same may be favorable.

We remain,
Correco and Brivio

Proceedings of Royal Commission to Inquire into the Immigration of Italian Labourers to Montreal and the alleged Fraudulent Practices of Employment Agencies (Ottawa, 1905), p.51.

An American inspector discovered that the firm of Correco and Brivio carried on a large-scale recruitment of unskilled labour in Italy for North American employers. They operated on the border of Switzerland and Italy. The town of Chiasso there rivalled Naples as a port of egress from Italy. Correco and Brivio were the owners of a sham "Swiss Emigration Society." They were also general agents for the Compagnie Generale Transatlantique and Beaver Lines which later was controlled by Canadian Pacific. Frederick Ludwig of the Swiss Emigration Society was jailed several times by Italian authorities for inducing Italians to migrate. Ludwig corresponded with *padrone* and labour agents in Montreal and Toronto who were, in turn, in the pay of hiring agents of the Canadian Pacific and Grand Trunk railways. A man named Fares operating out of Marseilles provided Greek and Syrian navvies in much the same way. Although Italian authorities had imposed stringent control on recruiting and shipboard conditions for Italian emigrants by 1901, they could not aid those who left the country through Chiasso or Ventimigilia and crossed the Atlantic from Liverpool, Le Havre or Bremen.

Immigrants arriving in Acton, outside Toronto, c. 1905

As to whether or not emigrants are induced to ship to Canada, who would otherwise have shipped to the United States, by reason of a cheaper fare or because of the $2 head tax, I respectfully submit that such immigrants are frequently, and in a large number of cases, induced to ship to Canada. The reason for this, however, is not the desire to avoid the $2 head tax, but because of the cheaper railroad fares charged to emigrants in the Dominion of Canada by the Canadian Pacific Railroad. In every such case the emigrant is invariably told that upon landing he must state his destination to be some place or town in Canada, where he intends to settle. Having thus availed themselves of the advantage of a cheaper fare, they then await the coming of an agent or some person connected with the agency where they purchased their tickets, and are escorted across the border into the United States.

Report of Special Immigrant Inspector Marcus Braun (1903) in B. Brandenburg, *Imported Americans* (New York, 1903), p.297.

Pieces of paper were crucial to the immigrant. Legal migrants from Italy needed a *nulla osta* (a notarized statement from village authorities that there were no obstacles to their leaving) and a passport. If Jews, Chinese, or Macedonians could not legally get papers to emigrate, they needed cards and scraps of paper that showed them the way through the maze that led to successful clandestine emigration. "Most emigrants are in possession of cards of all kinds of boardinghouses, emigrant agencies, and 'Homes' of all nationalities." Some carried slips of paper with the names of border guards who could be bribed on them; other bits of paper contained the address of a relative or a fellow-countryman who had gone to Canada before them. Railway and government authorities in Halifax pinned tickets and notes to the immigrant's clothing and warned them that if the bits of paper were lost, they would be lost.

Official or unofficial, intelligible to the immigrant or not, the bits of paper and documents made the "commerce of migration" work. Italians coming to Toronto by way of Ellis Island carried the address of an Italian food store in Buffalo. If they did not show it on arrival in Buffalo, the storekeeper-*padrone* did not find them work between Welland and Toronto.

Far right: Immigrants with Canadian Pacific Railway tickets in their hatbands

Below: An immigrant planning to return home also needed special papers

Right: Both sides of an immigrant landing pass

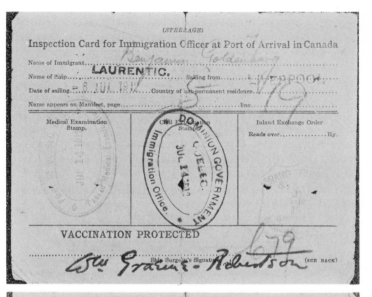

20

In the first place we find the only people who rigorously fight for these wholesale schemes are the Canadian Pacific Railway, the Grand Trunk Railway, the Dominion and Provincial Governments, the Salvation Army, etc., backed by all the big manufacturers, bankers, shipping rings and in fact by all those gentry who get much for nothing.
Jack Canuck (Toronto, December 30, 1911), p.10.

The newspaper *Jack Canuck* spoke out against the importation of migrant labourers on behalf of Canadian skilled tradesmen and unionists. In its anger and its hostility, though, it brought together populist and nativist sentiment against the immigrants and it made a telling point against Canadian big business. Since the 1890s the Dominion government had encouraged the immigration of certain nationalities as settlers. Parallel to the official government system of encouragement which favoured farmers and north Europeans, a "commerce of migration" had grown up. Steamship agents, labour bureaus, contractors and railway superintendents were drawn together in a network, the purpose of which was the exploitation of southern and eastern Europe's manpower. Shipping agents made their living from the bounty they received for each passenger; labour bureaus served as banks, boarding-houses, and middle-men for migrant labourers from Europe. The Canadian Pacific Railway and its sub-contractors depended on fresh shipments of migrant labour from Europe — Italians, Macedonians and Ukrainians particularly — to maintain low wages and a docile work force. Other labour-intensive industries followed suit, even sending immigrants back on paid holidays so that they might induce and shepherd over fellow-countrymen.

The immigrants, as peasants, were accustomed to being mistreated by bureaucrats and employers; they were less capable of understanding the hostility that they encountered on racial grounds. When the diffuse national feeling against "Romance, Slavonic and Oriental" people was combined with the native Canadian work force's fear for its job security and the natural clannishness of the newly arrived migrants, the situation at work sites was sometimes ugly. The system of labour recruitment could mean that a man might find himself isolated in a bunk car, serving as a strikebreaker at a site (the name of which he did not know), while angry native Canadian strikers threatened him. Such occasions encouraged the migrant worker to return to his homeland or to escape to the relative safety of a city like Toronto.

2 SHELTER AND STREET LIFE

Shelter was the prime concern of the newcomers. Arriving from southern and eastern Europe, few of them were prepared for the severity and length of the Toronto winter. They had little money, no access to credit, and only rudimentary knowledge of the country and the language. So they were often relegated to the worst housing in the city. Congregating in areas on the moving margins between industry, commerce and private residences, they found buildings and yards, potentially of great value, whose owners had moved out in the face of urban growth and the immigrant tide. These owners were prepared to turn their properties into high-density, low-maintenance housing for the newcomers, while they waited to sell to institutional and commercial developers. In time, wave after wave of immigrants found themselves crowded into buildings that were formerly one- and two-family homes, and even the sheds in the lanes and alleys "teemed with foreigners."

Toronto had a number of such neighbourhoods (see the map on page 27). The most important, located in the north and central portion of St. John's Ward, soon became known simply as "the Ward."* From the 1890s on, the Ward was a foreign immigrant receiving area. The largest new group in the Ward were Jews from eastern Europe, but they lived side by side with a large number of Italians. In the southern part of the district, Chinese, Poles, Finns, Ukrainians and other newcomers coexisted with the Jewish majority.

For those whose image of an immigrant neighbourhood is the shadowed and vertical world of Montreal or New York, the Ward, at first glance, would have appeared much less crowded and noxious. Of Toronto's immigrant poor, few inhabited tenements or multi-storey railroad flats; no cotton mills or elevated street railways loomed over their homes. From a distance, the northern reaches of the Ward, except for an occasional tenement, looked very like one of those squalid shanty towns that grew up on the verges of unincorporated mining camps and railroad sites. Here the newcomers crammed into the one- and two-storey houses, many of them frame or roughcast.

* The Ward was roughly the rectangle bounded on the north by College Street, on the south by Queen Street, on the west by University Avenue, and on the east by Yonge Street. As a neighbourhood, it was under constant assault from the hospital development starting in the northwest quadrant and from the growth of commercial and municipal property in the south and the east. When Agnes and St. Patrick Streets were connected to become Dundas, and when Terauley became an extension of Bay Street, it was obvious that the area could not survive as a residential neighbourhood.

In the laneways Italian and Jewish ragpickers piled their inventories. The absentee landlords made no effort to improve sanitary facilities, and drinking water often came from backyard wells. It was natural that the area took on the image of a running sore. The muck-raking newspaper, *Jack Canuck*, campaigned against the City Health Officer and warned of the typhoid danger in the foreign quarter. City services were minimal and grudgingly offered, while social workers and evangelists equivocated between calling for reform and trying to cleanse the aliens of their "squalid ways." Few people went in search of the absentee landlords and exploitive entrepreneurs who made the situation possible. Over 80 per cent of the stores, homes and rooms in the Ward in 1900 were rented.

The Ward was not the only staging area for the new Torontonians, and the overcrowded cottage in a mews was not the only form of congestion. Those national groups that had a much higher proportion of men to women in their migration (among them the Macedonians, Chinese, Greeks, Italians and Ruthenes) at first tended to live in boardinghouses near the railroads or other job sites. If they were joined by their families or were fortunate enough to have settled kinsmen, they moved into the Ward or they boarded with families in one of the other foreign quarters of the city. Such settlement occurred in a number of locations. Macedonians lived near King Street and Eastern Avenue; other Slavic immigrants had begun to reside along Queen Street East and near the Toronto Junction.

The worst extremes of boardinghouse crowding occurred amongst bachelor immigrants. Their ignorance of the country, their sense of themselves as sojourners, and their desire to save as much money as possible either for the purpose of returning to their homelands or of bringing over relatives made them easy prey for the greedy.

In contrast to the dour indoor life of much of downtown Toronto, the foreign quarters, particularly the Ward, had a very busy street life. Some of this activity could be attributed to Old World village habits of gathering, making conversation, and assuring the flow of information and gossip in a pre-literate society. The large variety of small traders and street vendors also made the streets the centre of life. Whether it was to watch an Italian with a trained bear, listen to a Macedonian Baptist preacher, or buy fresh vegetables, the immigrants moved easily into the streets. The non-linear streets and alleys of the Ward and the people idling or working in its streets made the area seem much like a European village. So it became Toronto's symbolic "foreign quarter." But, behind the colour in the streets lurked an ugly reality; for it was the overcrowded and dark interiors that encouraged street life.

None of the other neighbourhoods where newcomers congregated were as visible to Torontonians as the Ward. The other receiving areas were not situated so centrally that "a rear tenement under the morning shadow of the City Hall [was] occupied by six 'families'." Shack towns near the freight yards could be avoided by the genteel citizen and the Macedonians and other Slavs who lived east and west on King Street, away from the retail areas of the downtown, generally encountered Canadians and Britons of the working classes. Warehouses, factories and commercial establishments were interspersed with the settlement areas. The Italian neighbourhood that grew up after 1905 to the west of the Ward between the rectangle formed by Dundas, Grace, Manning and College Streets seemed foreign and cramped, but the houses were well kept, and the area lacked the decrepit and squalid aspects of the Ward.

Official concern with immigrant areas was expressed in 1911, when the city's Medical Officer of Health presented a report on a "Recent Investigation of Slum

Conditions in Toronto." Dr. Hastings chose six districts to investigate; three of them — the Ward, the area around Eastern Avenue, the Niagara and Spadina area — were districts containing large numbers of foreign immigrants. The report was phrased moderately but it assumed a connection between filth and foreign immigration, even if it did not blame the victims. "There could be no greater fallacy," the doctor wrote, "than that which so many people are labouring under, that people inhabiting slums are happy in their environment and not desirous of change." While condemning the landlord's greed, the report added that the assessed value of an acre in the Ward was over $100,000. It was unlikely that a landlord would spend for repairs to wretched old buildings on such valuable property. "From an economic standpoint, then, is it reasonable to think that the mechanic and the labouring class generally can be housed to as good an advantage on land of this value as on land in the suburbs which is assessed at from $1,000 to $2,000 per acre?"

Obliteration of the Ward and the dispersal or assimilation of its people became the logical course for the city's guardians. The litany that Dr. Hastings recited — contaminated water, overcrowding, windowless rooms, unsanitary water closets, filthy lanes and alleys, cesspools rising up through the back lots—called for obliteration as a response. Despite the Hastings Report, city officials, naturally enough, noticed the failings of the immigrants and not the city's own failure to provide services or control the landlords. In a Protestant society where God and cleanliness on the one side and the devil and microbes on the other seemed to be locked in endless Manichean struggle, "neutral" reports like that of the Medical Officer widened the gulf between old and new Torontonians. Scares about typhoid, cholera, scarlet fever were always linked to the immigrants. How many Canadians of the 1920s harboured an unconscious belief in a relationship between impetigo, poverty, and foreigners in their mind?

Even most of the social workers and evangelists who were working on behalf of the immigrants confused the physical and economic problems of the Ward with questions of assimilation. They were social workers not socialists, operating within the context of evangelism and Canadianization, not social reform. They saw the presence of foreigners as a challenge to religious and social normality, just as the inner city itself was. The modern city was a "sink of iniquity" and in the middle of the sink were strange men—Italians, Jews, Macedonians, Chinese, Syrians and Ukrainians. *Missionary Outlook*, a Toronto Methodist publication, described the problem starkly: "Every large city on the continent has its four-fold problem of the slum, the saloons, the foreign colonies, and the districts of vice . . . ."

Since the Ward was linked in the public mind with such urban pathologies, attacks on what was alien about the neighbourhood and what was simply impoverished about it became confused, while the undesirability of either condition became interwoven. Somehow an assortment of foreign storefronts, new church congregations and social clubs was equated with crowded immigrant housing conditions and the general uneasiness the "natives" felt about the new languages heard in the streets. So the reason offered for the obliteration of an immigrant area was obscure. Was it to break up forcibly the concentration of foreigners and thus to hasten assimilation, or did it have no other motive than the extirpation of unsafe housing conditions and unsightly commercial blocks? The answers lay deep in the consciences of those involved in the campaign to destroy the Ward. Writing in *The Canadian Magazine* in 1909, Augustus Bridle gloated over the counterattack against the neighbourhood being made by the Hospital Board's decision to expand the Toronto General Hospital facilities. "Jews and Gentiles fled the streets and lanes at the approach of the invader . . . . The Ward had a reputation for dirt and disease and diligent microbes. The Hospital was the enemy of all.''

So the living conditions of the newcomer and the areas that were considered immigrant neighbourhoods changed, partly because of the constant onslaught against cheaper housing in the centre of Toronto. Whether it was to make way for new commercial development, or for the spread of public institutions, the marginal housing of the immigrants and of the native poor was first to go. At the time, few people understood the complicated processes that caused a new ''foreign colony'' to grow up. Contemporaries assumed that cheap unsupervised housing and ''fellow-feeling'' created such districts. That explanation contained a partial truth, and it meshed well with the assumption that an immigrant neighbourhood was an urban pathological problem like slums or saloons.

The Ward's role as an immigrant area had followed naturally from its location. It lay directly north up York Street — an artery early crowded with boarding-houses, labour bureaus and low-rent shops — from the railway station. It was also, as it were, the backyards and laneways of the main commercial area along Yonge and Queen Streets. Thus it was near to work opportunities for small tradesmen and proprietors as well close to transportation for migrant labour gangs. There was cheap housing, absentee landlordism, and non-linear and unpaved streets. The growth of other foreign districts was less easily explained. Newcomers had little money and little English, so they did not wish to travel long and expensive hours to their employment. It was almost as if small company towns like those in the Ontario north evolved in the city. This explains the Macedonian concentration near the railway yards in the east end and the other Slavic areas around the stockyards and abbatoirs near the Junction. Few, if any, of these outlying areas developed sufficient commercial or street life to challenge the Ward's pre-eminence as Toronto's foreign quarter.

In fact, after the First World War, the Ward was no longer the only centre of Jewish and Italian life in the city. In the garment district around Spadina Avenue and in the Kensington Market area to the west, there was large-scale Jewish settlement and commerce. Italians began to settle to the west along College and Dundas Streets around St. Agnes Church. These areas had had some immigrants since the first decade of the century but after the war they served as the receiving neighbourhoods for newcomers as often as the Ward did. The development of institutions along University Avenue had driven many people to seek new homes, but the sequence and causes of the immigrant's moving westward are not clear. The destruction of the Ward's housing in favour of hospital space, the sewer work westward along College Street and the completion of the Dundas Street work caused Italians to move westward to the College-Manning area. Yet there were several Italian grocers and fruit dealers in the area before there were other Italian residents. Were those proprietors the pioneers who drew the others? Was it St. Agnes Church that drew them or did the parish become Italian in response to the new settlement? In 1901 Kensington Place, the core residential street in what was to become the Kensington Market area, was 80 per cent Anglo-Canadian; by 1911 it was 100 per cent Jewish. Why? Did the market area attract Jewish immigrants or did the residents faithful to their dietary ritual create the market? We can only suggest the internal causes of immigrant settlement patterns. The role that prejudice, changing commercial and street railway patterns also played in the development of the city's immigrant settlement is even more complex. Although some of the more extreme situations of poverty and overcrowding disappeared as the Ward itself was destroyed, immigrants still received less than adequate shelter in other parts of the city unless they became homeowners.

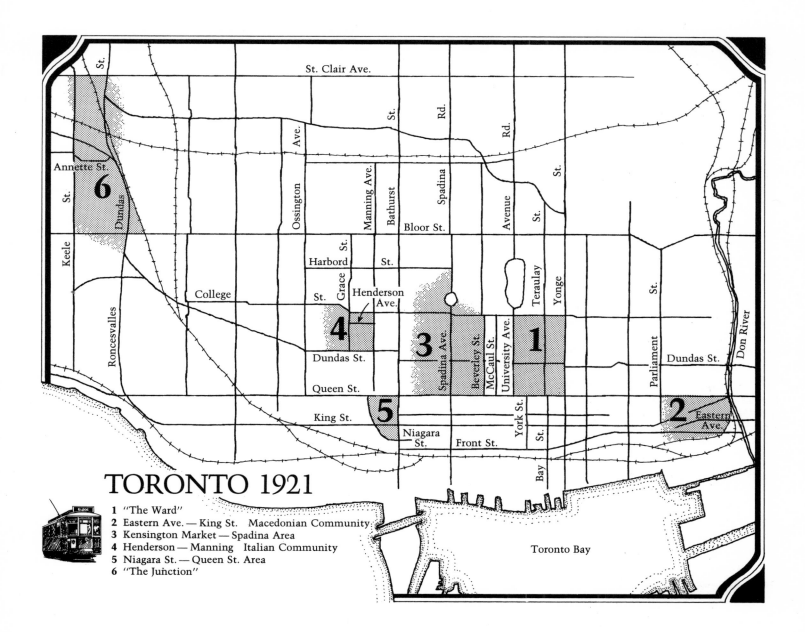

TORONTO 1921

1 "The Ward"
2 Eastern Ave. — King St.   Macedonian Community
3 Kensington Market — Spadina Area
4 Henderson — Manning   Italian Community
5 Niagara St. — Queen St. Area
6 "The Junction"

Innumerable tumbledown shacks stand in a state of slatternly decay, on both sides of the street. You peep inside one or two. For the doors stand ajar, letting in the dust from the street. And some air too, let us hope. Although one wonders how the air from that part of town can be worth coveting. Inside one of the doors, you catch a glimpse of a little girl rocking a sick baby. The room is tiny but contains a cook stove, a table, two or three chairs and an equal number of beds. Beds, undoubtedly, but from all appearances piles of filthy rags, thrown in indiscriminate piles on the floor.

Margaret Bell, "Toronto's Melting-Pot," *The Canadian Magazine* (July 1913), p.236.

Immigrant families when they first entered the city found housing through those of their own nationality who had come before them. A shack or a one-room apartment in the Ward was like steerage on shipboard, part of a longer process of migration. For those who wished to make money and return home, sinking most of one's wages into property was nonsense. For those who needed to raise passage money for loved ones left behind, the difference in rental costs between a one-room shack and a decent flat might cause the pre-paid ticket to lose its race against the next pogrom. In other words, until the immigrant family or the migrant had finished the journey from one country to another, housing in Toronto had to compete with more important items in the budget. This frame of mind was the real key to the pace each immigrant set in his or her escape from the receiving area.

A specific cause of crowding that particularly disturbed post-Victorian Toronto was the taking in of boarders, kinsmen or people from one's home town. The Hastings Report described a three-room house that two families lived in. "The middle room is divided by a low partition into a windowless kitchen used by both families, and a small living and sleeping room for the other family, a man, his wife and one child." In another house thirty-five people occupied twelve rooms. The Methodist Mission complained that it could not get Italian women out to attend social functions and language classes until the spring of the year. Before that they were too busy cooking and housekeeping for their families and their *bordanti*. Unused to the close extended family and strong hometown ties of the newcomers and assuming that the newcomers concerned themselves only with their well-being in Toronto, Canadians misunderstood the reasons for crowding in the Ward. They saw moral laxity, sloth and clannishness where there was often a ferocious determination to improve one's lot in this country or the Old Country.

Row houses in Toronto, 1905

There are no tenements in the "Ward" in the real meaning of the word. Families are, for the most part, housed in small buildings. The land is evidently being held for future speculation and in the meantime, landlords are making no improvements or repairs. As a result the families, with the exception of some of those owning their own homes, live in houses which leave much to be desired.

What is the "Ward" Going to do with Toronto?, Bureau of Municipal Research (Toronto 1918), p.23.

The Ward had the highest percentage of rough-cast and frame houses in the downtown area. "The common type is rough-cast, which begins in a shack flat on the soil with the doorsteps next to the sidewalk . . . . The squat one-storey frame frequently gets next to it; also abutting on the sidewalk, or separated from it by a mere strip of trampled clay." In many places windows were boarded-up doorframes and window sashes sagged.

The Bureau of Municipal Research undertook a thorough study of conditions in the Ward during the First World War. The Bureau, a non-profit institution funded by business interests and private contributors, came into being in 1915 as an urban research centre and as a lobby for better civic government. The report matter of factly blamed conditions in the Ward on absentee landlordism, speculation, and high property assessment on unimproved buildings.

While the Bureau understood the reasons for crowding, unsanitary housing and poverty in the Ward, its report did include a series of "Family Histories" which tended to show the immigrant residents as partially at fault for their conditions of life. Profiles of twenty immigrant families were taken from social workers in the Ward; the impression that this insertion left was that most families in the area had poor morals, poor health, and no initiative. If the reader assumed these family histories were typical, the report's introduction clearly warned him that the spread of foreigners meant the spread of all the unpleasant conditions in the Ward. "As a matter of fact, however, not only is the inhabited part of 'the Ward' becoming more congested, but it is boiling over into adjacent areas and new 'Wards' are springing up sporadically in other parts of the city as a result of the same economic and social forces which produced the parent 'Ward'."

Bottom right: Jewish immigrant family in a laneway behind Centre Avenue, 1912

Top right: One-room dwelling in the Ward, 1912

Below: Dilapidated rough-cast houses in the Ward

Next to the tenement house for condemnation is the one-roomed dwelling. The people of Toronto, or foreigners coming into Toronto, should not be permitted to be forced into such habitations. As Sydney Webb expresses it, "the soul-destroying conditions of the one-roomed dwelling which makes decent life impossible, involves the absence of proper light, air and privacy, leading to physical and mental suffering and inefficiency," must not be permitted in Toronto.

Report of the Medical Health Officer Dealing with the Recent Investigation of Slum Conditions in Toronto (Toronto, 1911), p.17.

In the Central District that included the Ward, 609 of 2,051 families had baths, but by far the worst problem was the plumbing and sewerage systems. Rear houses in the lanes were usually side by side with privy pits, box closets, and drain closets. In many instances windows could not be opened because of the stench. One immigrant woman remarked that she could see six privies from her kitchen window. Where shack housing had been built in lanes, backyards literally became cesspools.

Below: A visit from the health office on Spadina Avenue, 1916

Right: Interior of Jewish immigrant home, 1913

Whether tenement or one-room shack in the mews, the real problem of housing in the Ward was the state of repair of structures used as shelter. The immigrants made particularly supine tenants for speculators; they often feared or did not know how to seek redress of housing problems. Indeed, there were few remedies that would work without causing them more distress. Complaint might bring down city inspectors upon the house and lead to eviction. The daily report (record of services rendered) of social workers of Central Neighbourhood House in the Ward always included attempts to help tenants either with landlords or with the city.

In 1916 out of a total of 1,346 occupied buildings in the area, 1,141, or 85 per cent, were occupied by tenants. Landlords, since the value of the land was out of all proportion to the rents they could charge, were not particularly interested in the appearance or sanitary condition of their premises. For example, while frame cottages in the laneways off Elizabeth Street rented for about $12 a month, the value of land on the corner of College and Elizabeth Street rose from $95 per foot in 1909 to $1,000 per foot in 1917.

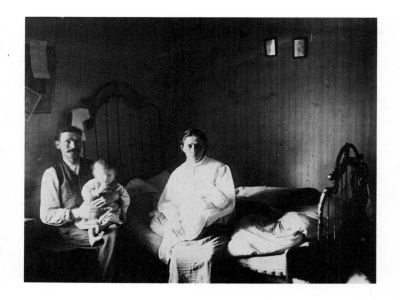

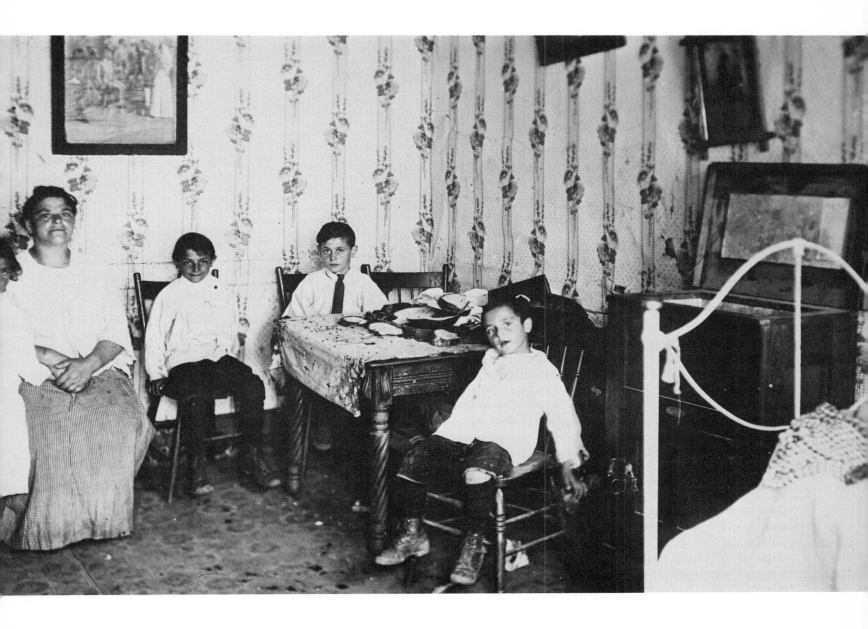

34

A couple of years ago, the Medical Health Officer of the City, Dr. Hastings, gave a great impetus to the movement for better housing in the country by his reports on slum conditions in the city of Toronto. He had certain districts investigated; and what did he find? He found 447 persons living in basements, 42 in cellars, 48 in houses with dark rooms. In one case, 19 men slept in three rooms, and in another 7 men slept in a room seven by twelve.

Rev. A.G. Sinclair, "The Family at Home," *Address to the Pre-Assembly Congress of the Presbyterian Church of Canada* (Toronto, 1913), p.166.

Below: Shift workers resting in boardinghouse on York Street, 1911

Right: Interior of Macedonian boardinghouse, 1913

Overcrowded lodging houses and inns were not an immigrant problem in and of themselves. In an expanding urban area before the development of apartment houses, most unattached people found lodging ranging from "room and board in a respectable home" to "workingmen's homes" and "missions." At one level at least, not perhaps a physical one, boardinghouses for bachelor immigrants were more normal and happier places than the shabby hotels and inns where wandering Canadian unskilled labourers lived. Immigrants, like the Macedonians in our pictures, had camaraderie and the bonds of language and fellow-feeling to ease the pains of overcrowding, dirt, and transience.

None the less, the worst extremes of crowding occurred in boardinghouses. Contractors or labour agents in the service of apathetic or insensitive Canadian firms led their men to boardinghouses that were little better than prisons. Dozens of men shared gloomy cell-like rooms, and in some places the changing work shifts kept the same beds warm for twenty-four hours of the day. For the really transient, though, rooming houses and inns were a winter home while they waited for the thaw to seek work in the interior. So extreme cold, gloom, lack of cash, and idleness must be added to our picture of overcrowding.

The rears of the dwellings are in even worse condition than the other surroundings. Here carelessness and untidiness seem to hold full sway. Rags and unused clothing lie scattered about, mingled with broken pieces of furniture, tin cans, broken stovepipe, and other junk, without any danger of being disturbed by the residents.
What is the "Ward" Going to do with Toronto?, Bureau of Municipal Research (Toronto 1918), pp.27-28.

The Bureau, like Dr. Hastings in his report on slum conditions of 1911, confused two problems. They equated dirty and unkempt property with sloth or neglect. That was only partially true; sometimes the disorder in the yard had nothing to do with landlord neglect, immigrant culture, or inadequate city services. The truth of the matter was that the clear distinction between domicile and place of business in the North American city was a fairly new development; men from small towns and villages — whether European immigrants or rural Canadians — did not always see the distinction. For the immigrants, the distinction between home and work would have been an expensive and impossible luxury.

Jewish family in their backyard in the Ward, 1913

38

It must be remembered that the government is not carrying on a propaganda for indiscriminate emigration to the Dominion. No inducements are held out in any way or promises to emigrants of an easy time and a speedy accumulation of wealth.

Report of the Commissioner of Emigration in Great Britain and Europe (4 July, 1905) in *Annual Report* of the Department of the Interior (1906), p.50.

Of all peoples unwelcome at border crossings, the gypsies led the list. While ethnologists of the time were not sure whether the gypsies were a separate race or not, fear and prejudice against them was the heritage of all of western literature. Along with their reputation for rascality, they were from south-eastern Europe and dark-skinned. Immigration classified them with Syrians and Armenians as "Orientals." Despite all the impediments to their migrations, gypsies managed to reach Toronto and all other major Canadian cities. The gypsies were migrants by tradition and often multilingual, so they were able to survive in the face of suspicion and hostility. Moving about in family groups or small "tribes," their wagons or old cars appeared in and around Toronto at certain times of year. The river valleys along the Humber and Don were their favourite campsites and those who did not come into the centre of the city to do business spent their time fishing and making sweet grass and reed artifacts.

Other gypsies rented dilapidated store-fronts on York Street and around the City Hall area, where they ran illicit palmistry and fortune-telling shops or bought and sold cut-rate goods. In the public imagination, they were surrounded with an aura of petty crime — theft, prostitution and various confidence games — but the evidence against them was slight. Their migrant life style and stubbornly alien ways made them archetypes of the "bad foreigner" — the unassimilable, dangerous enemies of To-

ronto the Good. The other east European immigrants added to the stock of tales about them.

Gypsy woman at encampment near Humber River, 1918

There are seven children living in the little room, next to the grocery shop. And every night a much bewhiskered father comes in from his rounds of the lanes and alleyways.
Just now he is back in the few square feet of mud, at the rear of the one-roomed house. You see him. There is a side alleyway leading from the street to the few square feet of mud. This alleyway is the receptacle for the thousands of bottles which are gathered on the streets every day.
Margaret Bell, "Toronto's Melting-Pot," p.238.

Margaret Bell, in her account of the Ward, went on to a vicious calumny about Jewish rag-pickers, but her description of the scavenger's home and business site again reminds us that people from small towns or rural areas did not distinguish between residental and commercial property. Imagine that distinction having any validity on a working farm. There was also a tendency, encouraged by the city's neglect of the Ward, to lose sight of the distinction between public and private property. In the Old World that distinction tended to be the result of class differences rather than civic enforcement. The same *droit utile* that had given many peasants the right to till fields that they did not own under law enabled the new townsmen to appropriate public laneways and sidewalks for their inventories or wares. The city imposed by-laws about public property by caprice. An Italian fruit merchant or a dealer in iron and junk never knew when a policeman or an inspector might arbitrarily demand that a sidewalk display or discarded goods in an alley be removed forthwith. There is no doubt that this pre-urban approach to the use of city space added to the overcrowded and disorderly appearance of the Ward and other market areas, but, except to the extent that rag-picking meant that there was refuse

about, these aspects of overcrowding were not the causes of filth and unsanitary conditions that the landlord's and city's neglect of sewerage and human waste systems were.

Backyards used for both family and business purposes

42

The paving of the street should be completed. It would then attract more of the general traffic and thus tend to relieve the congestion which at present exists on Yonge Street. . . It would be of advantage to the city as a whole, on account of the central position of the district, to have all these streets completely paved, since, besides giving better traffic accommodation, it would tend to lessen the dust and dirt nuisance.
What is the "Ward" Going to do with Toronto?, pp.12 and 13.

The Ward, because of the state of neglect of its streets and the lack of wide thoroughfares, had become a self-contained rectangle in the city. In compensation for the wretched crowding of yards and back alleys — it was estimated that over 60 per cent of the area was covered with buildings in comparison with about 40 per cent in the rectangle formed by Bloor, Carlton, Church and Sherbourne Streets — the streets of the Ward had not surrendered to motor vehicle traffic or impersonal institutions. With yards cluttered with sheds and goods and playgrounds limited, the streets of the Ward were the centre of children's lives, commerce, and socializing. In fact, the Ward was a village or a collection of villages. Dirt streets, shops next to homes, people loitering — all things that were untypical and somehow wrong in a large North American setting — were right in a village or rural town. The same characteristics would carry over to the Kensington Market area after 1910. Women shopped for meals on a day-to-day basis; men lingered over coffee or sat on stoops during the heat of the day, and the children were everywhere. The segregation of function and daily routine, so characteristic of North American industrial society, only slowly imposed itself on the immigrant family. Slum or neighbourhood?

The question was never quite answered for the Ward. It is true that most immigrants moved on to better housing and paved streets, but something was lost as well.

Top right: Edward Street in the heart of the Ward, 1918

Bottom right: Peddlers, stores and shoppers in Kensington Market, 1922

Below: Outside a kosher market in the Ward, 1911

44

And there are plenty of women who pause to have a look. Women wearing variegated shawls over their heads, and women wearing nothing over their heads. Women carrying babies and women carrying chickens. Fat women and thin women. ... Grocery shops with big dishes of melting butter in the windows, meat shops, showing pounds of fly-besmirched beef and huge cakes of tallow, fish shops with piles of sprawling perch and lake bass. ...
Margaret Bell, "Toronto's Melting-Pot," p.240.

Daily shopping was an involved business that accounted for much of the street life in the immigrant neighbourhoods. Whether from a shtetl in the Pale or an Italian small town, a wife's responsibility — whatever other employment she may have undertaken in North America — remained centred around providing meals for the family at the most reasonable price. Haggling, sampling, moving from small shop to small shop before deciding to buy, were aspects of this responsibility. They were, of course, also the chief basis of communication for women outside of the family. Shopkeepers, particulary *paesan* or *landsmann,* were important sources of information; they were also necessary sources of credit in hard times. The manner in which storefronts and domiciles ran together in the Ward or in the Kensington Market area made it possible for women to combine shopping with social calls. Bonds that grew up between women of the first immigrant generation often rivalled those of sisters, and sometimes crossed national lines. It was in many ways the womenfolk who kept the neighbourhood intact and created its *ambiente.* Some Italian mothers scolded sons for being late to light the *Shabbas* fire of orthodox Jewish neighbours. In a sense the Ward, like a European village, was governed by conventions set by elders. No naughty child in the street escaped the censure or scrutiny of clucking old women.

Below: Street life in the Ward

Right: Mrs. Solomon at 7 Price's Lane, 1916

Overleaf right: A street in Kensington Market, 1922

Overleaf above: Merchants and peddlers in a Ward street

And we do not have to go six blocks away from Massey Hall, Toronto, to find a whole city-full — I do not say a Toronto full but a city-full — of people that are at any rate non-Anglo-Saxon, a large portion of them non-Christian, and a goodly proportion of them, whether non Anglo-Saxon or Anglo-Saxon, pagan in life.

Rev. J.G. Shearer, "The Redemption of the City," *Address to the Pre-Assembly Congress of the Presbyterian Church of Canada,* pp.171-173.

Right: Secondhand stores and steam bath on York Street, near City Hall, 1922

Below: Italian and Chinese shops at Bloor and Havelock, outside the Ward, 1918

There was a tendency to confuse the Ward as a commercial district with the Ward as an area of immigrant residences. Whether anti-semites or not, reformers and evangelists alike objected to the plethora of small shops and the hubbub of commercial activity that grew up around City Hall. It seems likely that few of those who protested against the Ward's existence could have articulated the differences between their objection to the rapid growth of the city and the appearance of foreigners, particularly Jews. At any rate, the Ward, situated as it was, was a visible alien presence in a highly homogeneous society, and it would have to pay with its life for this flaunting of its foreign-ness. The "drama of the slum as they have it in Toronto—by some old-country critics considered worse than that of the ghettos of Europe [was] in a fair way to working itself out," wrote Augustus Bridle in 1909. That was not completely true because many shabby streets of shops and some residential streets survived intact into the 1930s. What was true was that immigration families and immigation shopkeepers were beginning to break free of the receiving area. Away from the Ward, they were noticed less by those hostile to the immigrant and they themselves began to sense that they had finished their migration and settled.

3 WORK AND ENTERPRISE

At the turn of the century when Roberto Teodoro arrived in Toronto from his native Abruzzi, there was no work in the city for him. He did find a job at a remote camp of the Ontario Northland Railway. Other migrant labourers from Italy, Macedonia and Galicia fanned out from Toronto to work either in the mines or at railroad sites in Northern Ontario. Work on the Welland Canal drew many others to the Niagara peninsula. The jobs were lonely, seasonal and backbreaking. For the workers, laid off when the snow came, Toronto was winter headquarters; during some winter months, five or six times the number of men were in the city as were there in the summer. From boarding-house or railroad bunk car, they ventured forth to seek diversion or part-time work in Toronto.

The chief concern of many was loved ones left behind in Europe. Transmitting money to pay for mortgages and dowries, or perhaps a prepaid steamship ticket, ate up most of their summer earnings, especially since they very often dealt with unscrupulous "bankers" and "travel agents." It is often assumed that the southern and eastern European bachelors who came as migrants to North America were unskilled, that they were peasants or the sons of peasants who could only survive by brawn and bicep. In fact, that is only partly true. In almost all the countries of emigration, people from the farm village learned the apprentice skills of some trade. Jews from the Pale, south Italians, Slavs, Hungarians and Greeks often had the beginnings of a skilled trade to fall back on. Perhaps it would be cobbling or barbering or tailoring; sometimes it was only the peasant sense of handling perishable foods like bananas. But such skills, combined with entrepreneurial sense, were to create the first small merchants and storefronts of each immigrant section of the city. Few men were simply unskilled labourers; the same men who might be navvies in the summer were often peddlers, tinkers or street entertainers in the winter. More and more the city itself provided work for the so-called unskilled labourers.

The great fire of 1904 destroyed about eighty to ninety buildings in the downtown core, but housebuilding was already in a boom period before the fire. New building in the city in 1905 was 448 per cent over 1900, and the 1910 figure jumped a further 104 per cent. The newcomers did not break easily into the more skilled builders' trades even if they were skilled enough. The development of the roads, sidewalks, sewers and then the street railway offered work opportunities to men who had learned to work with rock and stone and earth since childhood. Many of them already

51

had long experience with excavating and track work in the Canadian north. Most of the migrants came from the *minifundia* of Europe—areas where, because of the over-division of arable land, farmers no longer had need of a plough; all they used was a hoe or a *zappa* (mattock). The very conditions of the land that they had left, conditions that had caused their emigration, provided them with experience in excavating and terracing that few North Americans had. Men like Roberto Teodoro were artisans, skilled workers in stone, whose skill meshed neatly with the emerging industrial city and its communication and sanitation networks.

Toronto's development as a modern city coincided with the mass influx of immigrant labour. The immigrant work gangs were a necessary precondition to the modern era in much the same manner as railway navvies had been ten or twenty years before. A great city could not be made up of dirt streets and outhouses any more than a great nation could depend upon portages, single track and occasional line shacks. Metropolitan government, services and transit were only feasible when that infrastructure had been completed.

Gangs of men, often working knee-deep in the muck of unpaved roads, became a familiar sight in Toronto. The rapid development of commercial life and the razing of the Ward's northern reaches to provide room for new modern hospital facilities provided more labour-intensive job sites. Nativists might complain that the foreigners took work away from native Canadians, but, in fact, no reservoir of manpower sufficient for the scale of the city's take-off existed in the Ontario countryside. Capitalists and businessmen found the foreigners hard-working, easily controlled and, at least initially, oblivious to unionism. It was easier to hire twenty or a hundred Italians or Macedonians through one of the *padrone* like Dini's on York Street or from one of the international labour bureaus. A foreman or *padrone* "of their own kind" kept them in line for the Canadian work supervisor.

It might be well to stop a moment here and think about the work conditions and the choices and dangers open to this labour force. Obviously, there was less government intervention in business in the 1900s than now, and there was less concern for the foreign worker. For the railway work, they had been chosen partly for their apparent cliquishness, their transience and their lack of Canadian roots. If such men acted up, they were simply dismissed from the job site; for a Macedonian or Italian in the northern Ontario wilderness that was the final deterrent to protesting corrupt labour practices.

The city was different. In effect, the contract system which had worked so well in the wilds for railroad sub-contractors was applied to the building of the city infrastructure. City government everywhere, caught between the unpopular raising of taxes and the need to build public utilities, opted for the contract system. The City Engineer found that he could hire a general contractor for road-paving or sewer-building and leave manpower and other problems to the contractor. The quality of the work had to be checked; the time and the costs of the city contract had to be met by the contractors, but the city had no responsibility for the conditions of work, and the wages were not their problem.

Conditions in the city were different both for the contractor and the worker. The boss had a labour pool near at hand in the city—immigrant neighbourhoods—that he did not have at a remote railroad camp; but the worker, too, was able to develop alternatives. Improvement in the work conditions was the result of these alternatives, not of municipal supervision.

So the labourer, migrant or settled, could expect little help from the employer, the Canadian government, or the nascent and pitiably small and sectarian social services that existed. In almost all cases, he was a marginal man in terms of the country he had emigrated from as well. The consular services of various governments, as they existed, were for the middle classes and men of commerce, not for those who travelled in steerage from one land to another. Could a Pole or Jew expect help from Tsarist officials in North America? Macedonians were not even recognized as a people except in Bulgaria and little help could be expected from there. South Italians of rural origin assumed that the upper-class northern officials of the Italian embassies and consulates in North America found them an embarrassment, and they were probably right.

We are accustomed to think of the immigrant as doing the heaviest work and the most noxious work in the industrial city; they also did the most dangerous work. Sometimes that work was perilous by its very nature or by the immature state of technology—as, for example, when Roberto Teodoro discovered that he could make a good living by planting explosives for railroads and quarries. Other times the work involved casualties, not because of inherent dangers, but because of the callousness of employers, the tendency to use "faceless" immigrant labour precisely because it reduced the public outcry over human losses while boosting the profits. The yearly reports of the Ontario Provincial Inspectors of Factories are a litany of crushed digits and severed limbs. Yet only the accidents that occurred in factories and on the railroads were recorded. The hundreds of injuries that forced temporary or terminal unemployment for contract construction labour and for piece-work employees in the needle trades rarely made the lists.

Along with the sudden accident, debilitating, body-destroying work was also frequently the lot of the immigrant. There was no insurance against the shortened life span and the decline into brutality which came with certain kinds of work. When describing work in the found-

ries, an inspector wrote that "there is no class of work more laborious and subject to such extreme temperatures as that of the moulder. And it is not surprising that each year the class of labour is becoming more scarce. The young men of today prefer to select an occupation that is easier . . . ." But foreigners could be found for the work. A young Polish immigrant, strapping and healthy, was dead of tuberculosis a few years after going to work in the foundry. Other men, particularly Poles, Macedonians and Ukrainians, worked in dye factories and abbatoirs where their lungs and health were soon affected. Rheumatism and arthritis were chronic problems for men who lived by manual labour. Immigrants who worked in sewers and factory cellars found their bodies knotting up and useless at a time when honest pensions were rare and social security unknown.

Along with the developments of city streets and services, the largest employer of immigrant labour was the garment industry. Men and women of every nationality, but with Jews and Italians predominant, worked long hours in the so-called "needle trades." Employers found that they could use the immigrants to avoid the capital investment necessary for mechanization and yet they could still meet the demands of the new mass of consumers. It is ironic that people trained in the small pre-industrial trades in Europe made possible the production-line store-bought product of North America. The bulk of newcomers were drawn into the labour-intensive factory system, a system that helped destroy the artisanate, whether foreign or native-born.

Although the Spadina area would eventually be the centre of the garment industry, at the turn of the century the production of clothing went on in many forms and in many locations in the city. The T. Eaton Company produced its own line of goods in one of the largest single shop structures. Elsewhere, men who had learned how to fashion whole suits with loving care from the patient master craftsmen in the Russian Pale or in Galicia now passed their day sewing collar pieces together; women who had learned sewing as a domestic skill from their mothers found that sewing drew them out of domesticity and into the factories or, if they were fortunate, provided them with piece work at home, so that the Ward itself became a centre of cottage industry activity. Children of the immigrants faced an educational system and some social agencies that often appeared to believe that dexterity with a Singer sewing machine was the highest aspiration such children should have.

When compared to the muck and heaviness of outdoor work, dressmaking may have appeared to be light work, but it was by its very nature hard and exacting. The piece-work quotas, the tough foreman and the competition between small companies made it even harder. The Inspector of Factories found that "women engaged in it are liable to have to work over time more frequently than in other trades." Work areas, particularly in the smaller loft operation, were as full as fire and other laws permitted. Ventilation and light were poor. Employers consistently tried to avoid the costs imposed by a provincial ruling that there be enough washrooms for employees and separate facilities for men and women.

Vitiated and fetid air hung in the lofts during the winter. The floors were covered with dust, cuttings, expectoration and other health hazards. Only the cigarette and cigar-making factories — another trade dominated by immigrant labour—were more crowded and their air more unpleasant.

It becomes obvious from this account why so many immigrants struggled to free themselves from the peonage of factory or street labour, and why such a remarkable variety of immigrant enterprise began to emerge in the city of Toronto.

The early stereotype of the unskilled navvy grew from the need for immediate work and from the migrant nature of the first labourers. But there were other ways to make the money to survive in North America and to return to Europe or send for loved ones. Illiteracy and ignorance of the English language should not be confused with lack of intelligence and the initial dependence on menial jobs should not be confused with lack of enterprise. By 1921, 23,000 of 26,000 foreign-born Jews spoke English. The rapid growth of English among the immigrants was accompanied by the opportunity to break loose from factories, rag-picking and railway work and to try their chances as tradesmen and proprietors. Delivered from the virtual imprisonment that the isolated railway and mining towns had imposed, joined by wife and children, able to invest the small amounts accumulated by the sale of tiny farms or small shops in eastern or southern Europe, the immigrant was able to use his skills, his family cohesion and enterprise to compete in North America.

The way in which the immigrants could bring their skills to bear, the ways that they could find to make a living, were tied to the changing realities of the city economy as well as to the structure of prejudice. To a certain extent the immigrants could create their own economic opportunity, but only in so far as they kept their place within the larger society. Put simply, the newcomer could make money either directly from the new country, or he could make money from the other newcomers.

No easy class dichotomy exists between the immigrants who became entrepreneurs and those who remained labourers, factory hands and seamstresses. The same men who dug trenches or sewed collars might try their luck at night or when out of work as fruit peddlers, rag-pickers, or dry-goods salesmen. The man who opened a small shop in front of his home as a tailor or cobbler might not be more skilled than the "boy" stuck in the shoeshine parlour or the man in a loft sewing pieces all day. From the same house in the Ward, brothers sallied forth in the morning—one to work as a street cleaner (*spazzino*) another to teach music, a third to run a fruit stand. Perhaps all their children would be professional, perhaps none. The point is that a definition of their parents or their social class would be inadequate. They did not fit North American class structure, only its stereotypes, and they still lived partially in a more ascriptive setting of the immigrant urban village. The one occupation typical of many early immigrants was peddling. Peddling was ideal as a supplemental occupation. A navvy in winter quarters could try his hand at it. The patterns of trade for the immigrant peddler in the city were as elaborate as those of the drummers who crossed the prairies selling notions and dry goods.

Peddling, tinkering and hawking were the best chance the immigrant had of breaking free from grinding poverty or routine and heavy work. While it is true that many men, particularly among the Jews, had been peddlers in Europe, it is equally true that many more men tried their hand at peddling or as wandering tinkers and repairmen for the first time when they got to Toronto. Few men, even among those who had sold or mortaged stores before emigrating, could afford a store and inventory when they first arrived, but many could afford the small stocks that one could carry in a drummer bag, pushcart, or wagon; they also could find earlier immigrants and others willing to be their wholesalers and to provide them with dry goods or other stock, sometimes on account, for sale in the areas outside of downtown. In the long run, it was by dint of physical exertion that a man became a successful peddler. He had to be as tough as any navvy.

Of course, peddling was not a peculiarly Jewish occupation. There were peddlers of many nationalities, and there were many who plied their trades as tinkers throughout the same parts of the city who were not peddlers. City directories tell the story of the apparently inexorable rise of Italian immigrants as fruit peddlers. The reasons for the trade's popularity and for their success are worth noting. Men who found themselves unemployed in the winter, usually near the railyards — men who came from areas of southern Europe, particularly Sicily, that were traditional centres of the commerce in perishable fruits and vegetables — saw an opportunity for enterprise. Again, it was by backbreaking physical effort that the first Sicilian "banana men" reached railroad sidings before dawn to buy fruit wholesale and to spend the long day hawking it in the outer reaches of the city. Over time the more successful peddlers and pushcart vendors became middlemen and shopkeepers. Initially their only edge on their native Canadian competition was their willingness to go to the customer, to give the emerging Toronto middle classes the same custom service that had been the privilege of the rich. The efflorescence of peddling changed the city for the immigrant and for the older citizenry alike. Along with the road systems and the sewers, it gave those who moved into the inner suburbs, away from the downtown, all the comforts of the downtown. It led logically to the movement of many immigrant tradesmen away from their first settlements into new neighbourhoods. The clientele's goodwill meant that it was profitable for the Chinese laundry, Italian fruit store, Slavic cobbler, Jewish tailor or sundrys merchant to follow the middle-class flow.

So far we have dealt with the immigrant tradesmen or businessmen in terms of their relationship to the receiving society. As we have noted, there was another way to rise into the self-employed, to be a free man—by serving or exploiting fellow immigrants. To a very large extent, the success of these men lay in the nature of the old country connections retained by their fellow immigrants. In the early years, at least, it was unlikely that one could serve more than one immigrant group, although in certain aspects Poles, Jews and Russians shared needs and services.

For every group, there was a certain number of basic services and commercial possibilities. The clustering of ethnic shops created the *ambiente* of an immigrant neighbourhood. Such areas gave the lie to the crude stereotypes held of each group of newcomers by the larger society. Chinatown was not all restaurants and laundries, a ghetto was not all junk peddlers and tailors, a "Little Italy" was not cobblers and ice cream stores. These shops were there but they were flanked by a rich assortment of establishments serving many more aspects of the immigrants' needs of body and soul. The first successful businesses were those that dealt with the migrant work process itself—steamship agents, labour bureaus, and inns for bachelor workmen. The importing or production of familiar Old World foods followed. The steamship agents imported staples such as pasta, rice, salt fish and tomato paste. In an age before supermarkets, the Ward seemed to have a variety or grocery store on every corner. Soon the local manufacture of foods competed with the importers and provisioners.

Men of every nationality ran restaurants or cafés that were essentially for their own kind, especially for the bachelor workers. Such places were also haunts for the menfolk in the evening, substitutes for true cafés and taverns. Barbershops within the immigrant neighbourhood also served as community centres, and the space in front at night could look like a village square.

The Jewish immigrants, more than any other group, developed a large number of enterprises to meet their own needs. The *kashruth* (religious dietary laws) and the traditions of being a self-contained minority encouraged the proliferation of speciality shops. Certainly the line between shops in the Ward or Kensington Market that served the Jewish community and those that were ancillaries to the garment, hardware or scavenger businesses was not always obvious. But in every immigrant group, a very significant number of businesses emerged not just to provide the food needs of their people but also as adjuncts to their ritual life.

Very often, after initial hostility or fear, establishments created for the needs of one immigrant group became chic gathering places or just downright sources of good things for other inhabitants of the city. Italian fruit vendors and large Jewish and Italian bakeries, just because of the superiority of their goods, changed the home-eating habits of much of the older stock. Chinese and Italian restaurants around Dundas and then around Elm and Gerrard Streets created something akin to tourism within the city. At first the lure of the exotic in the form of spaghetti and chop suey had traces of prejudice and thrill-seeking, but before long such restaurants were natural and central institutions of the city. Macedonians, not with their own cuisine necessarily, came to run restaurants all over the city, ranging from the elegant dining room to the hunble dinner.

A few hard-working immigrants who purchased the buildings where their businesses were located found that they owned many of the city's most valuable properties, and so immigrant families prospered through their frugality. By the end of the First World War, many immigrants and their children had gone beyond earlier stereotyped occupations to participation in the larger capitalist economy and assimilation. Doctors, dentists, government clerks, lawyers, were appearing in every group by the 1920s. Many of them retained their immigrant identity and found their clientele within their parent's community.

Perhaps with careful and detailed study, historians will be able to show that the immigrants, with their anxiety for work and their small skills, provided the take-off for industrialization or even a substitute for it in the early years. The immigrants helped to bring creature comforts to the Canadian middle classes at low cost and without disruption of genteel society. Packaged cigarettes, cement sidewalks, paved roads, trolley systems, factory-made clothing, all depended on immigrant labour. In that sense, the expansion of the city itself from downtown to the inner suburbs depended on the immigrants.

58

As a rule, a good percentage of them are absent from the City during some months in the year. A number have been employed in the new bridge being built near Brockville by the Ottawa and New York railroad; others have recently gone to work on the railways near Hull, Muskoka and Niagara Falls, and a good many others have been employed on the Peterborough canal.

"Foreigners Who Live in Toronto," *Daily Mail and Empire*, October 21, 1897.

The city was a place from which to sally forth in search of work; it was also a place to fall back on when employment was scarce, and men were unable to return to their homeland. The work site might be five hundred or a thousand miles away from Toronto, but the Ward or a neighbourhood like it, remained the base camp. It was the address to which relatives sent mail. In Toronto were the importers of Italian foodstuffs, the boardinghouses where migrant workers left messages for each other, and the offices of the steamship agents, labour bureaus and immigrant bankers who transmitted funds back to villages and towns in Europe.

Although he spent much of his life in the hinterland, working as a navvy and later a skilled quarryman, Roberto Teodoro considered Toronto the place to which he had emigrated. He used some of his hard-earned wages to pay a professional photographer for a picture to send back to Chieti in the Abruzzi. With two other Italian navvies, he posed in his Sunday best to show the people back in southern Italy that their sons were healthy, prosperous, and had the companionship of *paesani*. By posing together, the three friends could send the good news to three families at one-third the cost. Such photographs, perhaps accompanied by a prepaid ticket, could bring out a wife from the old country and change a man's life.

Roberto Teodoro and two friends pose for a picture to send home, 1911

I was unable to obtain direct information as to the exact nature of the operations of these steamship agents in Italy, but from such information as I was able to gather, and believe to be reliable, I am inclined to think that many of them should properly be considered as fraudulent employment agencies. They get a commission on tickets which they sell from the transportation companies, and, it has been represented, charge in many cases a higher rate of transportation than they are legally entitled to; they collect also in some instances fees from intending emigrants for information which they give in regard to means of securing employment on this side.

Report of Deputy Minister of Labour, *The Labour Gazette,* June 1906, p.1,348.

The steamship companies preferred the south European passenger trade since the high rate of returnees added income and ballast on the return trip to Europe. The flow of people in a peak year like 1907 was over 200,000 in each direction. Hamburg Amerika Lines had at least five steamers dedicated exclusively to the Italian trade. Clandestine emigration from Italy through Chiasso usually led to passage on Beaver Line or the Compagnie Generale Transatlantique. With migrant workers transmitting over 75 per cent of their wages back to the old country and the system of prepaid tickets, steamship agencies naturally became informal banks and employment bureaus as well. "All available space is filled with steamship posters, money-changing notices, and many coloured placards, alluring always in the inducements they present."

The man who had conquered the vagaries of English, could understand or circumvent the law, and had some sense of the labour situation, could become the most important person in the immigrant community. Such a man received respect without being trusted, but the migrant navvies expected to pay for the right to work and for the use of knowledge of Canada that the steamship agent had.

Italian business established on Agnes (Dundas) Street in 1910

The mission hall serves many other useful purposes, such as the Labor Exchange and Information Bureau, by means of which scores of foreigners are directed where they may obtain employment.
C.J. Cameron, *Foreigners or Canadians* (Toronto, 1913), p.46.

The group of Macedonian navvies are posed with the Rev. John Kolesnikoff, a Baptist minister who came from Pennsylvania to work among the newcomers in Toronto. The average age of the transient workers was quite young, as the picture indicates. For a minority of the workers, evangelists tried to organize their boardinghouse life and job opportunities. The majority who remained faithful to their eastern orthodox faith were just as young. When they gathered in 1911 to sign a protocol for the formation of a parish, elders were chosen from each village transplanted in Canada to collect the tithe for the church building. Of the twenty village elders chosen, only four were over thirty years of age. The youthfulness of the navvies and the fact that many of them thought not as individuals but as dutiful sons and fiancés sent to America with no other purpose than the saving of cash, made of them a very reliable work force. "He obeys the orders of the boss. He is not anxious to go on strike, as he counts that any increase in wages would in the short period he intends to remain in the country no more than reimburse him for the wages while the strike is on." The building of a church and the maturing of the migrants meant that they would become a more permanent and less docile work force.

Right: Macedonian saloon on King Street East, 1911

Far right: Young Macedonian workers with the Rev. John Kolesnikoff outside the International Labour Exchange on Eastern Avenue

Every keeper of a tavern, hotel, or boarding-house, in any city, town, village, or place in Canada designated by any Order-in-Council who receives into his house as boarder or lodger any immigrant within three months from his arrival in Canada, shall cause to be kept conspicuously posted in the public rooms and passages of his house, and printed upon his business cards, a list of the prices which will be charged to immigrants per day and week for board or lodging, or both, and also the prices for separate meals, which cards shall also contain the name of the keeper of such house, together with the name of the street in which it is situate, and its number in such street . . . .

Order-in-Council enforcing Immigration Act of 1908, *The Labour Gazette* (August 1908), p.187.

The boardinghouses and inns where migrant European workers spent their winter months resembled all too closely the shanties and bunk cars at their summer work site. Usually the boardinghouses were located near the railway yards and, although some were open to lodgers of every nationality, most served migrants from only one country. True sojourners wished to spend as little in rents as possible. Migrants were not uprooted; they purposely sacrificed in their Canadian life in order that they or their loved ones could live better in the country from which they emigrated. The boardinghouse enabled them to save while also retaining the *ambiente* of their homeland. An Italian evangelist complained about the boardinghouse-migrant syndrome. "But if their aim is to stay here only a few years, until they have accumulated some money, then they live worse than in Sicily, because there is no privation that they are not ready to endure in order to save money."

The city's response to the transient navvy was limited by its complicated and obsolescent welfare system and by the tempo of migrant work itself. By the time a particularly unpleasant boardinghouse situation came to the attention of officials, the boarders were often back in their country of origin or off working in the hinterland. Dr. Hastings' report on slum conditions in Toronto in 1911 observed the degree to which such boardinghouses maximized savings for the sojourner and profits for the settled immigrant or native Canadian who owned them. "Each man pays about 75 cents to $1.25 a week for lodging and washing, and the owner reaps a rich harvest. These are not poor men — they are in receipt of good wages, $1.75 to $2 a day . . . . Our inspectors have some evidence that certain small hotels and old and roomy houses are about to undergo the dangerous transformation into foreign lodging houses."

Boardinghouse on York Street, winter, 1910

66

The newcomers drawn by the factories will be of the poorer class, and will have to be provided by the taxpayers with their share of city services, and with an education for their children, the great growing expense of which, under the arbitrary demands of the school board, has caused a note of warning to be sounded by the Mayor; as well it may, when we have the expenditure of the Trunk Sewer, rendered more inevitable than ever by the increase of the population in view.

Goldwin Smith, "Toronto! A Turn in its History," *The Canadian Magazine* (April 1906), p.525.

Despite Goldwin Smith's hostility to increasing urbanization, most of Toronto perceived, if only dimly, that immigrant labour was intimately and complexly bound up with the city's growth. The middle classes of the inner suburbs were able to move beyond a system of outhouses and cesspools because immigrants worked under dangerous and abhorrent conditions to create a metropolitan sewer system. While Smith may have seen the trunk sewer as an expense born of an imprudent immigration policy, it was also noticeable that the last housing to feel the impact of the new system was in the Ward.

Sewer work carried the risk of noxious gases and sudden cave-ins. The safety extremes are obvious in our pictures of sewer workers. The building boom in Toronto in the 1900s did not immediately open the skilled trades to the immigrant, but the ancillary work of excavation, putting in water mains and, of course, the sewers provided work on a scale that enabled men who had been migrants, often seasonal railway navvies, to settle permanently in the city, to send for families, and to break with the boardinghouse cycle of life. Italians — because they often had experience in fashioning earth, brick and stone — dominated the excavation work in Toronto.

Immigrant sewer workers, c. 1912

There they are, a whole hundred of them, bare-armed, bare-necked, sturdy, brown fellows, forming a cordon in the middle of the street, between the two rows of tumbledown shacks which form the business section of the city's melting pot!

The picks swing up, then down, then up again. Each swing is accompanied by some utterance, an unintelligible muttering or a snatch of song. And you think of the Italian operas and the greatest singers of them. From such a melting-pot as this have they often come.

They do not pay much attention to you as you walk past. They would like to, you can tell, by the side-glances which are jerked toward you. But the boss is there in the midst of them. And the big clock on the City Hall is calling out the hour of four. There is much to be done before the street will be ready for the steam roller.

Margaret Bell, "Toronto's Melting-Pot," *The Canadian Magazine* (July 1913), p.234.

The spread of the sub-contract system from the railways to the city street work and the private street railways meant that immigrant contract labour, gangs controlled by their foremen, replaced the corporation worker on many urban work projects. Competition for city contracts was fierce and the contractors took their margin of profit out of their immigrant day labourers. Many foremen and timekeepers tried to swindle the workers; men were sent home without pay on stormy days, and of course they were not paid for the time spent going to and from the work site. Good pay for such a street labourer in 1905 would have been about $1.75 a day. Beyond the risk of being run down by train or trolley or maimed by unfamiliar machinery like the steam roller, there were also insidious dangers. Men who worked in marshy ground such as areas of the harbour and on the Welland Canal before settling in Toronto fell prey to recurrent bouts of malaria, the very condition that had led some to leave the lowland areas of their native countries.

Right: Track reconstruction on Queen Street, 1917

Below: Italian stonemason at work on Eastern Avenue, 1916

Gather the tools, boys. It is nearly six o'clock. Put them in the tool-box. Cover the cement. We have finished for the day. Tony, you attend to the red lamps; light them and put them in their places. The watchman will not be here till seven o'clock. He guards the tools and machines till daylight. The nights are cold in October.

A. Fitzpatrick, *Handbook for New Canadians: A Reader* (Toronto, 1919), p.49.

Fitzpatrick had founded Frontier College in the late 1890s. After the First World War, he produced a primer for the immigrant navvy. The English-language lesson chapters taught simple sentences based on the day-to-day encounters and work experiences of the immigrants. They also instilled stereotypes about the role of different groups in the work force. Under the sub-contract system particularly, work gangs tended to belong to a single nationality. Men were hired in gangs with a foreman of their own nationality in charge. It was not uncommon at a work site for there to be a "Canadian" boss and an immigrant boss standing side by side. The common nationality of work gangs was not just the result of hiring practices. It would have been downright dangerous to have linguistic confusion at a badly shored-up excavation site or when danger threatened a fellow worker who was unaware of it. More than once a Polish or an Italian warning of imminent danger had gone unheeded by a fellow worker who did not know their languages.

Far right: Street work on Wilton Avenue, 1903

Right: Laying cobblestones on King Street, 1903

72

David Gurfosky of Toronto sued the Lehigh Valley Railway Company for damages arising through the death of a relative. The action was dismissed on the ground that the deceased being an alien his family could not recover.
Labour Gazette (Ottawa 1906), p.943.

Before the First World War, the migrant or immigrant worker who was maimed or disabled could expect little help, particularly if he worked for a sub-contractor. Even the names of such men have disappeared; the payrolls of contract labour have not even survived. A man injured on the work site could expect only dismissal; if he belonged to an immigrant mutual aid society he might receive some benefits. Since most of the immigrants came from humble or rural classes or belonged to ethnic minorities in their country of origin, their personal contacts with consular officials from their homeland were not much easier than with the agents of the Canadian host society.

Men who had never worked with large-scale machinery had to work in close proximity with machines that lacked safety devices. Dangerous open gears, hot pitch, or falling concrete could be avoided, but for men who had little sense of electricity every stray wire, every electrical machine, and every sign in a language that could not be read held the possibility of instant death.

Far right: Terauley Street (later Bay Street), 1914

Right: City repair plant, Princess Street, 1926

An Italian and a Pole seldom see eye to eye when they happen to be sufficiently interested in each other to try it; and both exhibit little reluctance in filling up the chasm of conversation with a knife or pistol. The Swede prefers his fists, the Italian a knife, the Pole and Russian a revolver, and the Hungarian uses anything from a rock to his teeth.

W. Lacy Amy, "The Life of the Bohunk," *The Canadian Magazine* (January 1913), p.219.

Nativist images of the newcomers as quarrelsome, deadly, fundamentally transient, and mutually antagonistic prevailed long after the situations in which those stereotypes had originated disappeared. Railway and quarry sub-contractors had purposely pitted gangs of one nationality against another in order to encourage competition and keep the work force fragmented. Men who knew little of the language and had allegiance only to their own kind found themselves willy-nilly in the position of strike-breakers. Antagonisms were fiercest in isolated camps and mining towns; they declined in the city. Gentled by the presence of women and children, accustomed to other newcomers, the city immigrant worker was a far cry from the brawling and rough navvy of the bush. The end of a sub-contract system that had encouraged gangs of one nationality, and the appearance of less divisive hiring practices produced a heterogeneous work force, as this photograph from the Toronto Transit Commission collection was supposed to suggest.

Our pictures also show that some work gangs had the coherence that family structure and artisan skills created. In Europe, children often accompanied fathers to work in order to learn the family trade and add to the family income. Since much work in Toronto took place in the summer that practice continued here.

Left: Work on the Bloor Viaduct, 1918

Above: Toronto street railway work crew

In several places two or three sewing machines were being used in the manufacture of men's clothing. Some of these were in unsanitary places. In one house, as many as eight of these sewing machines were concealed.

Report of the Medical Health Officer Dealing with the Recent Investigation of Slum Conditions in Toronto (Toronto 1911), p.13.

Conditions in the needle trades ranged from those described above to the well-organized factory structure of the T. Eaton Company. The idea of sweat shops, of immigrant men, women and children working under unsanitary conditions on the upper floor of slum dwellings paradoxically co-existed with a belief that learning to use a sewing machine was a most useful thing for a young immigrant girl to do. Central Neighbourhood House and the missions ran dressmaking and sewing classes for the girls of the Ward. Given the economic conditions of most immigrant families, it is difficult to believe that such children did not more often sew collars for men's shirts than sew the patchwork quilts of settlement house fancy.

Since many immigrants had tailoring skills, the new piece-work and assembly-line methods of clothing production rested heavily upon them. Men working in a pressing room dreamed of having their own tailor shops, and the cutthroat piece-work system in some immigrant homes reflected aspirations and a family sense of the economy as much as it did exploitation. That the latter was equally true is eloquently testified to by the early strength of socialism among clothing workers.

Above: Pressing room as the T. Eaton Company, c. 1904

Right: Jewish tailors making Eaton-brand clothing, 1912

A. Tailors are, however, beginning to dispense with workshops and are allowing tailors to take the work home.

Q. Then the work is being done outside?

A. Yes.

Q. Are there any Italians doing tailoring work?

A. They take the work home, and they run what are know as sweating shops. They are making quite a pile of money, and have a few slaves under them in the shape of women.

Q. Do they work cheaper than regular men?

A. They do the work cheaper, and they get women to do the work cheaper still.

Royal Commission of the Relations between Capital and Labor (1889), Vol. V (Ontario Evidence), p.628.

Newcomers of every nationality became involved in the needle trades. Native tailors like the man interrogated above considered the immigrant tailors and seamstresses as intruders who threatened their livelihood. In fact, the decline of tailoring as an exclusively artisan trade was tied to the emergence of mass consumption and mass markets. The factory system employed unskilled or less skilled people of every nationality at the expense of the highly skilled of every nationality. The line between a tailor shop, a clothing factory, and a family sweat shop was not easy to discern. Government factory inspectors, for example, were never certain when they should insist that a shop have separate washroom facilities for its employees or when they should simply see everyone in the shop as a family unit.

The larger concerns such as the T. Eaton Company, beyond being the catalysts to unionization, had a profound effect on the immigrant social and cultural structure. Men worked side by side with women who were not of their family, and people of every nationality worked side by side in crowded areas or had to cooperate on assembly lines.

Below: Men and women working side by side at the T. Eaton Company, 1904

Right: Sewing loft in the city

Report #16 of the Committee on Fire and Light

Your Committee beg to recommend that Messrs. Cohen Brothers be granted permission to build a 59' chain oven in a basement factory in course of erection in the rear of a lot situated on the easterly side of Ontario Street, a short distance south of Queen Street.

Minutes of the Toronto City Council (September 1907), p.1223.

Food processing and cigarette/cigar manufacturing rivalled the needle trades as an occupation for immigrant workers. Many Italians from the Ward worked at the City Dairy. Others were cellarmen and lumpers in the city's breweries. Around the Toronto Junction, Slavs who worked in the abbatoirs had a thriving neighbourhood. The presence of the newcomers affected the food industry in several ways. The special food demands of immigrants combined with the efforts of peddlers and shopkeepers to increase the volume and variety of foods in the city. While it is true that immigrants did many of the most noxious and dehumanizing jobs in factories and slaughterhouses, the line between worker and proprietor, just as in the needle trades, was obscure. Many men of peasant background had routinely learned the art of the butcher; one year they might work in one of the large modern abbatoirs; the next they might try to open a meat market catering to the tastes of their countrymen.

The making of cigarettes and cigars was also largely an immigrant trade. Rolling quality cigars had been a highly specialized skill in Europe, but in North America the mass consumption of cheap cigarettes required a different kind of work force in both skill and status. Young women, particularly, got work as cigarette factory operatives. The rooms where the cigarettes were rolled were also the rooms in which the tobacco leaf was dry-cured at night. This meant that the windows were often sealed. Village people from southern and eastern Europe had often followed an agricultural routine that included a midday rest and a leisurely lunch. In the factory, they gulped down cold lunches amidst tobacco leavings or clothing scraps in order to meet their quotas or to leave an hour earlier in order to prepare supper for the immigrant family.

Some were more fortunate, for the demands of the food industry allowed specialists to pursue a lifestyle almost exactly like the one left behind. Chinese restaurants needed Chinese truck farms; Jewish orthodoxy required a ritual butcher; and a skilled cigarmaker could display his artisan skills comfortably from a shop window.

Below: Ritual slaughterer (*shochet*) preparing for work, 1910

Right: Cigar-maker in store window on Queen Street, c. 1924

82

They seem to be heralding something. In a moment, you see it. A man with a hurdy-gurdy and a dancing bear. One youngster more bold than the rest is throwing banana skins at it, and bits of orange peel and grape-fruit from the gutter.

They pause before a fish shop. The man has wonderful spangles on his coat and wears a peculiar shaped hat. With one hand, he turns the handle of the hurdy-gurdy, with the other, waves a vari-coloured baton, which seems to have a rattle in one end. The big brown bear circles round and round. There are shrieks from the mob of dirty faced youngsters. Fat shop women come out of their doors, and stand with hands on hips.

Margaret Bell, "Toronto's Melting-Pot."

About 1890, a man named Martucci brought the first street organ to Toronto. He came from England and was reputed to make from $10 to $15 each day in his first few years in Toronto. By the turn of the century, there were a dozen street-organ men in the city and profits were down. Some were accompanied, not by trained animals, but young girls or boys who were themselves musicians or singers. When Fiorello LaGuardia became mayor of New York City, he banned hurdy-gurdy men from the streets. He had been embarrassed as a boy when his father, a military bandmaster in the American southwest, had be-friended an itinerant organ-grinder. The elder LaGuardia understood that the occupation was an ancient and hon-ourable one; young Fiorello saw only the ridicule that went with the North American stereotype. Charles Dick-ens had found North American cities dull in the mid-nineteenth century when compared to London. "But how quiet the streets are: Are there no itinerant bands; no wind or stringed instruments? No, not one. By day, are there no Punches, Fantoccini, Dancing dogs, Jugglers, Conjurers, Orchestrinas, or even barrel-organs? No, not one." Before home radios and cheap theatres, the street entertainers brought a special gift to dour urban society. Their presence was a European amenity that North America never prop-erly understood. It was, as well, a skilled art form, and many street entertainers became music teachers in the same manner as peddlers became shopkeepers.

Street musicians, c. 1920

T'eatre out, people's come — dats so,
Apell sze peanut, see benan',
Six vive cent for's 'who buy?
I sell all so s'cheap as I can.

Thus night after night as I stroll down the street
At his cart in the corner the same man I meet,
At the southwestern corner of Ad'laide and Yonge,
Where the Saxon falls sweet from the soft Latin tongue.

W.A. Sherwood, "The Italian Fruit Vendor," in *The Canadian Magazine* (Toronto 1895).

Italians, Macedonians, Greeks and Syrians trudged many miles through unfamiliar parts of the city to sell peanuts, popcorn and homemade confection. A cart well-stocked with charcoal for the fire, cashews, chestnuts, candied apples or Turkish Delight was just as unwieldy and as heavy as a cart of bananas or dry goods. Sudden rain or an overzealous police constable could cost a whole day's effort, and that one day might represent the week's profit margin.

According to the *Daily Mail and Empire*, by 1897 Italians controlled "almost entirely the banana trade of the City and indeed have worked up a remarkable business in that line." There were over one hundred banana wagons in the city, and, in one year, "each of three wholesale houses in the city have provided them with from thirty to fifty thousand bunches of bananas." Bewildered by small boys, pilfered by passing cops, the push cart man managed to smile and chant "six banan' vive cent ... Ah, lady! sze 'Talyman's cheap ...." Was it his sunny Latin disposition, his sly caricature of his own stereotype, or his entrepreneurial spirit that kept the smile on his face? And did the stereotype held of him by the Canadian matrons in Rosedale help to sell his fruit? More fascinating still, had the fruit peddlers created their own market? Had Canadians included so much fruit and vegetables in their diet before southern Europeans showed them the range and joy of such food stuffs? Italo-Canadians to this day refer to some English Canadians as "mangia-cakes," cake-eaters, to imply the limits of their diets compared to that of the Mediterranean countries.

Below: Italian banana man on Roncesvalles Avenue, 1919

Right: Popcorn man, near Coxwell and Queen, c. 1922

Your Committee have received complaints from time to time regarding the means adopted by certain peddlers to sell their goods. It appears that they load a wagon with fruit or whatever else they please and drive along the main thoroughfares of the City hawking their goods much to the annoyance of the citizens, but the action more particularly complained of by store-keepers is the injury to their business by disposing of the very same kind of goods as they themselves keep in stock, at prices much less than they can afford to sell in view of the heavy rents and taxes imposed upon them.

Report #9 of the Committee of Markets and Licenses, *Minutes of the Toronto City Council* (1890), p.811.

Among the licences issued in 1907, there were 817 peddlers' permits, 41 for "petty chapmen," 508 for rag collectors, and 60 for second-hand and junk dealers. There must have been a large number of unlicensed small businessmen as well. Peddling came easily to all the immigrants; even if they had never tried it themselves, they came from the small rural villages and towns where the itinerant salesman was common. Many Jews from the small cities of eastern Europe had performed similar roles as travelling merchants for the little *shtetls* and Christian hamlets of Galicia, Poland and the Ukraine. They had dared to walk great distances amidst hostile people speaking a foreign tongue in the European countryside; they did the same in Toronto.

Why, as the Kensington area developed as a Jewish market, was there always one non-Jewish shop, a fruit market? Why in a neighbourhood of the northern Ward were all the peddlers Jewish except the ice cream vendor, the popcorn man, and the fruit peddler? Were there Italian dry-goods peddlers and Jewish fruit peddlers in any numbers. If not, why not?

Street peddlers

His fathers papers
Nat Dec 29/10

No. 124

CITY OF TORONTO

Pedlar's License on Foot

INDUSTRY INTELLIGENCE INTEGRITY

This License *is granted on payment of ONE DOLLAR to the City Treasurer, as hereunder acknowledged, to* B. W. Goldenberg

of No. 12 Russell *Street*

to authorize him to carry on the business and calling of a **Pedlar** *in the City of Toronto.*

This License to be in force until the 31st day of December, A.D., 1918

THIS LICENSE CANNOT BE SOLD OR TRANSFERRED

DATED this 19 *day of* March *A.D., 1918*

RECEIVED the sum of ONE DOLLAR

T. BRADSHAW, CITY TREASURER

PER E. C. Davenport RECEIVER

H. J. GRASETT

CHIEF CONSTABLE

We like those keen-witted little merchants of the streets — the newsboys, precocious, old too soon. Their manhood came down like a wet blanket upon their boyhood, and they never came to manhood.

An investigation revealed the fact that only one in four after he becomes a man, earned more that $4.00 a week . . . . It is the right of the child to have the long preparatory period of twenty one years . . . . A child of three years of age has no right to be kept at home sorting buttons; a child of five years has no right to be straightening tobacco leaves. A child of ten or twelve years has no right to be employed in any store of factory.

Rev. J.W. MacMillan, *Address to the Pre-Assembly of the Presbyterian Church of Canada* (Toronto 1913), p.160.

For the immigrants, the family was very often seen as a single economic unit. The differentiation of roles that the North American middle classes took to be a divine rule (i.e., that the man was breadwinner, the mother was homemaker, and the children students) was a luxury of those well-established in the land. Filial obedience and piety had been a part of the east and south European rural heritage: father and son harvested together; a son ran the shop while his father went to the city for supplies or to the countryside to buy hides from the peasants. While there was no doubt a brutal edge to child labour in the factory system, it was not parental callousness but a traditional way of looking at things that made all family members try to make money. There was some justification for the immigrant family to see the children of the older stock as monstrous and egotistical freeloaders upon the family structure. Italian consular officials in American cities commented on how immigrant parents regretted the fact that their children learned in school the individualism and selfishness of their North American classmates. It should be noted also that the age of manhood was considerably younger among Jews, Italians and Macedonians than among urban Canadians; this was a fact of rural life as well as a cultural value.

Far right: Finnish maids, c. 1915

Below: Newsboy

Right: Laundry worker taking a break, c. 1909

92

A white-coated man, with a brownish face, has paused at a corner. He rings a bell, and calls something half-English, half something else. He has a little cart. All the tawdry youngsters appear from their respective hovels, and run out to greet him. They fight and scramble, each intent on being the first to reach the cart. The brownish-faced man smiles. There is always a good market for his ice-cream cones among the dirty-faced youngsters of the Hebrew district.

Margaret Bell, "Toronto's Melting-Pot," p.240.

Despite the racism that makes "Hebrew" children "tawdry" and "dirty-faced" and the Italian ice-cream vendor "brownish-faced," this little account of an encounter in the Ward makes an interesting point. In the evening, peddlers, vendors, entertainers converged on the Ward from every direction; it was their home. They did not stop hawking their wares until they reached the threshold of their houses. The last "Miserere" on the street organ, the last attempt to sell some pots and pans, the dregs of an ice cream vat or a popcorn machine were dispensed in the Ward. Perhaps, it was this tired homing in the evening that eventually convinced men that they should open shops outside the Ward, that they should forego the ambience and take their chances among their Canadian clientele. The colour of the Ward in the evening was one thing, making a living another. Throughout the city, vendors of food, particularly fruit and confections of every kind, opened stores. The step from peddling to proprietorship was not just a sign that one's lot had improved substantially but also that enough acculturation had occurred or courage arisen to live in the New World, to cease to be migrant and portable.

Below: Serbian-owned candy store on Queen near Power Street, 1922

Right: Walerstein's ice cream parlor, Spadina Avenue, c. 1920

Overleaf: Kosher fishmonger

Overleaf right: Macedonian ice cream parlor

This is part of the drama which may be seen more completely in a stroll down Agnes Street after the play. Here is a shoptown, the most cosmopolitan part of Toronto; on cross streets and side streets the rows of blinking little modern shops . . . . In one block alone on a single street were three restaurants and three barber shops. Here were grocery stores and shoe-shops; fruit stores and wall-paper establishments — even a large bicycle repair establishment with fifty bicycles stacked outside, beside a number of Chinese laundries.

Augustus Bridle, "The Drama of the Ward," *The Canadian Magazine* (November 1909), p.6.

The nature of a man's trade did not necessarily relate to the pace of his acculturation or the nationality of his clientele. To say that there were so many Jewish or Italian barbers, so many Macedonian or Chinese restauranteurs is to say very little about the nature of those individual businesses, as these pictures should demonstrate. Some barbershops doubled as social clubs for a specific group of *paesani* or *landsmann*; the barber was the guardian of home country lore and gossip. Some restaurants and cafés fulfilled the same function, some even had meal tickets and a system of board for bachelors of a given nationality, while other restaurants were geared to a Canadian or at least a multinational clientele. Running a shop could be simply the continuation of one's existence in an Old World village or town, or a brand new experience. Bernardo's barbershop catered to Canadian businessmen; the barbers returned to their own neighbourhood at night for social life and perhaps loitered at another barbershop in the Ward that they used as a rendezvous. The owner of Bernardo's, although an accomplished barber, had apprenticed in Italy as a shoemaker. The label Jewish restaurant could cover anything from a place with kosher dairy products to a drugstore with a lunch counter.

The most visible newcomers were the Jews. Some of that visibility came, of course, from lurking prejudice in Canadian society, but the Jews were non-Christians in a Christian city, small-town people in a city, and east Europeans in a North American city. In the New World as in the Old, two basic Jewish community needs intertwined. There was the need to maintain the religious ritual of one's ancestors, and the need to find a *parnosseh*, a livelihood, in a society that ranged from neutral to hostile. The ritual needs themselves provided employment for a number of men. Meat, fish, and dairy products had to be prepared in the proper way, so in the Ward a new *shtetl* was born, rich in all the many trades that were traditional in the Pale. Kosher poulterers, *Shabbas* fish mongers, bakeries for *challah*, shops selling *tallith* (prayer shawls) and even a religious book store were the Old World transplanted in the Ward.

Right: Jewish shop in the Ward

Overleaf left: Meeting place in the Ward

Overleaf right: Bernardo Barbershop, Bloor and Yonge, 1920

Truly there is a great and varied assortment of goods outside that shop, most of them displayed in a pyramid of Hebrew disorder . . . .

Chickens seem to be the crest of all the Hebrew shops. On every window appears a paint-besmeared figure, which, according to the motive of the painter was supposed to represent a half-matured fowl. Both sexes of bird are represented, probably on account of the militancy of things amongst a sex of more civilized extraction.

Margaret Bell, "Toronto's Melting-Pot," p.240.

As the pictures show, "Hebrew disorder" ranged from the crowded informal hardware store to the beautifully arranged and enumerated goods of the clothing store. The concentration of Jewish shops in the area around the City Hall and in the Spadina area obviously caught the eye of those hostile to the Jews. The eyes of such beholders tended to miss the variety of enterprise and of relative prosperity among the Jewish shops. An anti-semite could not see clearly enough to distinguish between shops that served the Jewish community and those that were a part of the garment or housing industries. Anti-semites could condemn Jews for the marginality of their businesses while identifying them with capitalists like the Rothschilds. In fact, for the majority of Jewish immigrants in the city, business establishments were as small as they had been in the little shtetls of eastern Europe.

A dry goods merchant

Overleaf left: Sign over the premises of a ritual slaughterer, 1910

Overleaf right: Drugstore on Spadina Avenue, c. 1920

Overleaf centre: Hardware and tinsmith shop on Queen Street

104

Are the Chinese stores, laundries, and restaurants, so thickly abounding on King, Queen and York Streets which these unfortunate girls are alleged to frequent "dens"? If so why the tolerant attitude of our Morality Department towards them?

There are no less than 25 Chinese stores, laundries and restaurants in the blocks bounded by King, Queen, Yonge and York Streets. How many of them are "dens" in Police court parlance?

One need only stroll through the above mentioned blocks and notice the throngs of Chinese lounging in the streets and doorways to realize that the "Yellow Peril" is more than a mere word in this city.

Jack Canuck, September 16, 1911, p.10.

Chinese ran laundries throughout the city and a concentration of Chinese business establishments and restaurants existed around the City Hall area. The greatest rancour toward newcomers in the city seemed to be directed against the Chinese, despite their generally law-abiding and unobtrusive social behaviour. Partly, of course, antagonism was fanned by the national attention given to the exclusionist campaign in British Columbia, but anti-Chinese feeling had local roots as well. The radical and muckraking newspaper *Jack Canuck* carried on an anti-Chinese campaign for many years. The census of 1911 counted over a thousand Chinese men and thirty women in Toronto. A good part of the reason for hostility to the Chinese may lie in that statistic. Forced by a harsh head tax imposed by the Dominion government to leave their women behind, the Chinese lived in bachelor groups. Perhaps because of their own guilty Victorian fantasies, a section of Toronto opinion, fed on *Jack Canuck* letters to the editor or lurid missionary accounts about opium and white-slave traffic, saw the Chinese as a threat to Toronto society.

Chinese businesses in the centre of the city

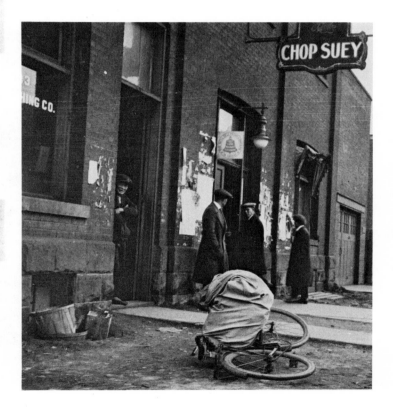

Glionna, Donato grocer 249 Chestnut
—, Donato tailor 144 Chestnut
—, Donato fireman Drill Hall
        72 Elm
—, Egidio musician
        176 Chestnut
—, Francis foreman 5 Percy
—, Frank musician
        217 University Ave
—, James music teacher
        57 Elm
—, Vincent hotel 144 Chestnut
—, Vincenzo Glionna-Mariscano
        Orchestra 57 Elm

Mights Toronto City Directory, 1904

All immigrant groups had more variety of enterprise and more mobility than our pictures can suggest. Whether among their co-nationals or in the larger city, men found new economic opportunity. For example, Little Italy in the Ward had streets crowded with shoemakers, tailors, little groceries, travel agencies, hotels, inns, and music schools. There were also bakeries and confectionaries. In the Eastern Avenue area, Macedonian bakers, fruit and food stores, artisan shops, and boardinghouses existed. From such a variety of pursuits, profits were made and new enterprises and careers begun. One Italian family in the Ward in 1904 counted nine adult males: their occupations included a grocer, a tailor, four musicians, a foreman of street work crews, and the keeper of an inn. In 1912 the grocer was still a grocer but lived outside the Ward; the tailor was an immigration officer; the musicians led a well-known and successful orchestra and a music school. The foreman's son was an officer in the Customs House and later an independent customs broker. Another family in 1904 had four adult males: a shoemaker (employed by a large firm), a labourer, a fruit peddler and music teacher. By 1912 the same family was involved in a real estate business and a billiard parlour. As they left the railway work and settled in the city, Macedonians became involved in restaurants, bakeries, ice cream parlours, and shoeshining establishments as well as tailor shops and shoemakers' shops. Heads of Jewish families who were listed as rag-pickers in 1904 were merchants by 1911.

Traditional skills and trades brought from the old country

4 EDUCATION AND THE CANADIAN WAY

The foreigner, and more particularly his children, came to regard Toronto as home; but many older Toronto residents had doubts — doubts whether the foreigner could ever be anything but a foreigner, doubts whether the children of these people would prove anything but aliens in this land of their adoption. The photographs in this chapter explore the life of children and parents caught between a home where Old World ways remained entrenched and a new world of classrooms, settlement houses, social workers, street life and dreams of the future in which the Old World often seemed sadly out of place.

A potential for conflict was always present. How could it be otherwise? But more often than not, parent and child alike gradually recognized the unending tension between the parents' way and the Canadian way to be an unavoidable fact of life, part of the price one paid for re-settling in the New World. In the classroom, for instance, the immigrant child was rewarded for his efforts in English and punished for reverting to his mother tongue. At home the English language was an intruder who won increasing acceptance among children, but more slowly among parents. The very word, "English," often became an adjective used to describe objects, events or customs of the en-croaching outsiders: English bread to describe soft-crusted white bread so popular among "Canadians," English holi-days to denote national or religious holidays which might close schools and banks but have no place in the foreigner's home, and English clothes to describe the very store-bought attire often made in local factories by these same immigrants. The English were the real Canadians.

The English world was never very distant. The child who owed his parents filial loyalty confronted a teacher who demanded a new national loyalty; to prove his would-be Canadianness the child was encouraged to prove he was different from his parents—to think, act and speak "English," "White" or "Canadian." Parents might be con-cerned, but it was a concern moderated by uneasy ambiva-lence. They generally recognized the importance of educa-tion, acknowledging that facile use of English eased one's existence; they hoped, however, that their children could go through school and acquire the new language without giving up or rejecting the other values of the immigrant home.

The official task of Canadianizing the foreigner fell to an unspecified coalition of educators, civil servants, social workers, religious leaders and public health officials. With rare exceptions, these guardians of the Canadian way worked with but one goal in mind: to remake the foreigner

109

in their own image. For some the task was a veritable Pygmalion effort. One speaker at the 1913 Pre-Assembly Congress of the Presbyterian Church in Toronto explained, "The problem is simply this: take all the different nationalities, German, French, Italian, Russian and all the others that are sending their surplus into Canada; mix them with the Anglo-Saxon stock and produce a uniform race wherein the Anglo-Saxon peculiarities shall prevail."

Rather than "Anglo-conformity," transforming the foreigner into a model Anglo-Canadian, some talked of an American style "melting pot" in which all peoples and cultures would blend to create a new and dynamic Canadian man. In an impassioned speech before the 1912 Ontario Educational Association meeting held in Toronto, a speaker predicted: "The Canadian nationality of the future will not be English, French, Latin, Teuton or Slav, but rather a combination of all of these, with the virtues and vices that are peculiar to all."

Yet this difference in imagery, melting pot versus Anglo-conformity, proved to be more a difference in rhetoric than in vision. To proponents of assimilation by whatever name, the foreign issue boiled down to one simple problem — Why can't they be like us?

The older generation, already set in its ways, was sometimes dismissed as beyond the possibility of Canadianization. In 1918 a University of Toronto researcher conceded, "Their hearts will remain, to a very great extent, bound up with the scenes of their childhood." However, if adults might remain beyond full assimilation, the teacher, social worker and settlement house volunteer regarded their children as more malleable material.

While compulsory school attendance laws prodded the few reluctant parents, the vast majority of foreigners dutifully, even enthusiastically, bundled their children off every weekday morning to study. Teachers, principals, inspectors and school board members, for their part, envisioned education not just as the process of learning but, perhaps more importantly, as the process of *becoming*. Under their watchful eye those children were marked for transformation from foreigners into useful young Canadians. From the morning's ritual opening exercises — the singing of "God Save the King," a salute to the flag, reciting the Lord's Prayer and usually a short Bible reading — until class was finally dismissed into the streets in the later afternoon, schools emphasized the Canadian way, a way which an educational spokesman defined in 1907 as "punctuality, regularity, obedience, industry, cleanliness, decency of appearance and behavior, regard for the rights of others and respect for law and order." The formula was recited as if none of those values animated the immigrant home. One teacher stated more simply, Canadians are "tidy, neat and sincere" — foreigners are not.

Canadianization was not a hidden curriculum. Teaching of the Canadian way permeated every facet of the school's program. The three R's proved no exception. The working of a routine mathematics problem sanctified growth, progress and competitive business practices. Through the study of literature, reading materials promoted nationalism and Protestantism, often as if they were one and the same. As late as 1928, Toronto's Chief Inspector of Schools boasted of one institution, "The teachers of this school are teaching English to their students, but they are also not losing sight of the broader aim, the Canadianizing of our foreign population."

The school's Canadianization work extended beyond the formal classroom program. Students were encouraged to look to schools for assistance with personal problems and planning for the future. In technical, commercial and academic streams teachers or counsellors supplemented parents as a central source of information and advice. There seemed so much about Canada that parents just did not know, could not understand. The parent who could not himself move confidently into the Canadian mainstream could not long hope to be an unchallenged source of guidance on the Canadian way. Thus, schools inevitably undermined the influence of the home. Parents, already viewed as strangers by the outside world, were increasingly being relegated to the position of virtual strangers, beloved but hopeless foreigners, in the eyes of their own children.

The neighbourhood schools returned children to the streets in the late afternoon. Here in the streets, however, the children of foreigners were again sought out by the guardians of the Canadian way. School Canadianization efforts were complemented, in some cases surpassed, by the work of settlement houses. Offering an atmosphere far more relaxed than that of the schools, settlement workers reached out into the streets, into the neighbourhood parks and playgrounds, to gather the children of foreigners for late afternoon and evening activities.

The three Toronto settlement houses working in areas of heavy foreign concentration, St. Christopher House, University Settlement and Central Neighbourhood House, were staffed by small teams of trained social workers supplemented by a dedicated body of volunteers. Although each of these Toronto settlement houses was equally committed to Canadianization, they differed from one another in tone. Most notably, Central Neighbourhood House, unlike its two sister houses, was nonsecretarian, owing no allegiance to any Protestant church. It trod a thin philosophic line between forceful assimilation as the best method to ensure the immigrant's adjustment, and respect for continuity of ethnic identity as to the best method to prevent social breakdown in the New World. In practice however, all three settlement houses saw eventual and complete Canadianization as desirable and inevitable.

Like the schools, settlement houses worked to minimize the influence of the home or, at least, overcome what was seen as its shortcomings. Unlike schoolteachers, settlement workers confronted the home directly, sometimes in the most tragic of circumstances. During 1918, for instance, in an era before the introduction of our present public social service networks, Central Neighbourhood House workers alone visited approximately 3,400 homes. Most of these calls were simply regarded as "neighbourly visits," but a large number were not. "Juvenile and parent delinquency, illness, desertion, poverty, cruelty, ambition, ignorance of the language and customs of the country and many other causes" presented problems for the workers to try to solve.

Problems involving children proved especially trying. Settlement workers periodically confronted the outrages of child labour — not just in daytime factory or retail store jobs, but in the employment of children as late-night newspaper boys, pin-setters in night bowling alleys and, in rare instances, as prostitutes. On such occasions as seemed necessary, settlement workers functioned in loose alliance with police, truant officers and court officials to attack these pernicious social evils. Of course, such problems were functions of poverty and not of ethnic or immigrant origin. Child labour of certain kinds, for example, had the tacit approval of Canadian society. The daily visitation sheet of a social worker from Central Neighbourhood House showed as much trouble with child labour in the homes of the native-born and British immigrant as among "foreign" elements.

While the settlement house offered assistance and guidance at an immediately personal level, the bulk of its activity among foreigners involved organized group work, especially among the young. A social worker explained, "It is primarily the children and the young people that the House aims to help, and it is through them that the parents are influenced to adopt better, cleaner,

Canadian ways." As one might expect, the twin pillars of service education and health care were given prime attention by the settlement houses. Studying English, acknowledged as the most important of many social and intellectual requirements necessary to assure complete acceptance by Canadians, was directed by volunteers. In contrast, health services, often developed in cooperation with municipal health authorities or public institutions such as the Hospital for Sick Children, were largely the preserve of the professional. Baby clinics, distribution of milk and cod liver oil, instruction of mothers in child care, visiting nurses, organization of open air camps and day outings with money contributed by the *Toronto Star* Fresh Air Fund were carefully planned and generally well received. These health services were not just lauded by community workers for their impact on the physical health of the community. In 1913 it was claimed that health services also offered "the first step toward making possible the Canadianization of the immigrant and his or her total conversion to our national standards of life, methods and morals."

Schools, settlement houses, the streets and the countless interactions children had with the outside world undoubtedly had their effect. In short order most children learned English and moved more confidently, more widely and, as often as not, more invisibly in that English-speaking world which lay beyond the home than did their parents. In this regard children took on new importance. For the newcomers and "greenhorns," an English-speaking child became virtual ambassador to the outside world, privy to family secrets and exposed to issues normally deemed beyond the understanding of a child. It was left for the children to complete forms for this or that government agency, explain to the visiting nurse or the doctor at the free hospital clinic about a mother's abnormal discharge or unravel the mystery of printed immigration regulations.

As a result, parents were often forced to reverse traditional roles with their children. Rather than the child being dependent on parents, non-English-speaking parents found themselves dependent on their children.

Time and continued contact with the "English" would gradually allow most parents to become functionally conversant in the new language, but seldom without a self-conscious search for that elusive right word, seldom without a thick accent which assaulted the native speaker's ear and begged imitation by the vaudeville comedian. A series of English-language night school classes for adults offered some assistance. In addition to night classes organized by the public schools and local settlement houses, Protestant missions to Jews and Catholics emphasized English-language instruction. Missions wished to make it possible for the would-be convert to read the Bible in English, to break the foreigner's dependence on his home, church or, following a broader assimilationist theme, to "Canadianize the foreigner by Christianizing him."

The process of Canadianization did not go unchallenged. In an effort to slow the forces of assimilation, in an effort to channel youthful energy toward a pride in traditional language, culture or religious heritage, many foreigners sought out their kinsmen and their co-religionists in order to organize their own classes. For some, like the Jews, the mandatory afternoon school, the *Chader*, with its emphasis on religious study, preparation for Bar Mitzvah and participation in Jewish communal life was transplanted from Europe, but not without modification. Forced to compete with settlement houses, schools and the wonders of a late afternoon in the park, the *Chader* was often seen by children not so much as a centre of Jewish learning as an obligation many Jewish boys felt they had fulfilled on their thirteenth birthday.

Jews were not alone in organizing communal schools. In cramped rooms at the back of a church where priest and parishers spoke the same language as the home, many Greek, Italian, Finnish, Ukrainian, Chinese and Macedonian parents organized classes for their children. Unlike the Jew, however, these foreigners had no Old World *Chader* for precedent. In the old country there had been no need. There children learned to read, write and appreciate the mother tongue, to perform the rituals of religious life, as naturally as they learned to walk. Here things were so different. Public schools promulgated Anglo-conformity beyond the classroom. If the mother tongue was to be preserved, religious traditions sustained and a sense of group consciousness developed, immigrants felt they had to support their own afternoon and Sunday schools — no matter the cost, no matter how meagre seemed the results.

In part because Canadianization did not go unchallenged, it is probably impossible to measure with any exactness the actual success achieved by the crusaders for assimilation. How can we ever know for sure whether teachers, social workers or visiting nurses played as great a role in Canadianizing the foreigner as they claimed, as they might have hoped? We can be sure, however, that the teacher, missionary, visiting nurse and social worker regarded Canadianization, especially of children, as a process with one clearly identifiable goal—the moulding of a new man out of an Old World clay. Within one generation, two at most, the assimilationist believed the process would be complete; immigrants would be Canadianized and their strange ways be only an historical memory.

In part they were right; it was unavoidable that children of foreigners should look beyond the home, beyond their parents, for visions of tomorrow. With formal education the Italian, Jewish, Finnish, Hungarian, Ukrainian or Greek child was promised a chance to grow up as a Canadian. Social workers and educators sincerely believed, and children were repeatedly told, that Cinderella was not a fairy tale—it was the essence of a New World dream.

Yet, for many the sense of being a Canadian has not meant either melting pot or Anglo-conformity. It has meant the development of Canadian life in which traditional immigrant roots, family customs and religious beliefs have not been masked away but refined to complement a changing Canadian way.

If Canada is wise, she will profit by the mistakes of her neighbours to the south, and see that the immigrant encouraged or allowed to settle in this country is not merely left to his own to sink or swim, but is led to feel that the country is glad to have him, provided he conforms to the laws, sends his children to school, takes an interested pride in his new country. But he must have educational facilities good and cheap, and must be protected from unfair exploitation.

J. Murray Gibbon, "The Foreign Born," *Queen's Quarterly* 27 (1920), p.350.

Brant Street Public School playground was surrounded by a brick wall. Once inside the compound, all sight of the surrounding neighbourhood was blocked off as boys and girls played separately under the supervision of a teacher. Most of the children at Brant Street School were the children of immigrants. Some had themselves been born abroad. Any given classroom in the school might well include Jewish children who lived along Queen Street, Russians and Poles who lived in the rented flats dotting Carmen and West, a few Italian, Finnish or Chinese children who lived on Oxley or Brant Street itself.

Paul Sherman (second row, second from the right) was a pupil at Brant Street School. He was born in Toronto a few years before his sister Minnie. They lived together with their parents and three brothers and a sister on Queen Street only a few blocks from the school. The Shermans were financially better established than most of the families who sent children to Brant Street School. Paul's parents, Russian-Jewish immigrants who entered Canada after the turn of the century, established a hardware store. The family lived above the store and still had enough space to take in tenants. They also had indoor plumbing, a fact which might help to explain why Minnie's teacher on one occasion was able to remark to her other pupils, "Why can't you children be clean like Minnie?"

It was the store, however, which dominated and "Canadianized." It was not just a business but also a local institution dispensing standard hardware supplies and such now-exotic items as coal oil, a cure for lice, and *bunykis*, the small glass containers used in cupping blood to the surface of the skin as the remedy for a variety of internal pains. Perhaps because of the store, the Sherman family was functionally bilingual. Although parents spoke to children in Yiddish and children answered in English, both languages held equal status in the family business. In this they were different from many of their classmates. English-language instruction was central to Brant Street School's curriculum, as it was in all schools with large immigrant populations.

Unfortunately, few special English language classes existed. As a result older children who did not speak English were often placed into classes with much younger children. Here, it was reasoned, the level of English usage was so sufficiently simple as to allow these older students to learn English quickly. The process accelerated the drop-out rate far faster than it did formal English-language learning.

Brant Street Public School, c. 1920

116

In the last few years Toronto has received a great number of immigrants from nations not Anglo-Saxon. So great has been this influx, that we have now in this city a foreign population of about 70,000.

If these people are to be assimilated and made good citizens, it must be largely through education. The Board of Education realizes this and provides liberally for these people.

The progress these pupils make is marvellous . . . . The children are industrious, intelligent, respectful and obedient; they are exceedingly appreciative; they have that greatest incentive to effort, viz. feeling the need of what you are after, and their progress delights the teacher as it is so visible and rapid.

Toronto Board of Education, Chief Inspector's Report, *Annual Report*, 1913, pp.28-29.

Optimism and a sense of mission dominate many reports from those who worked with the children of foreigners. Educators who saw the classroom as the laboratory in Canadianization naturally applauded a child's natural and rapid ability to assimilate the English language. They interpreted language facility as both an endorsement of existing educational methods and a sure sign of the child's enthusiasm for everything "Canadian." Children, however, had priorities all their own. If they were "industrious, intelligent, respectful and obedient," they were also cautious. Of necessity they learned that the behaviour demanded of them in the school, reinforced in manual training classes where potential job skills were refined, was not necessarily welcomed in the home or the street.

At home, industry, intelligence, respect and obedience were also honoured, but not necessarily the same way as they were in the school or would be on the job. To the foreigner, industry, punctuality and regularity were seldom measured by the clock, intelligence was not something to be learned in books, respect was more than deference and obedience extended well beyond a momentary willingness to accept authority. The child had to balance often conflicting values or differing behaviour associated with specific values at school, at home or, sometimes, on the job. Yet, it was this very juggling act, with all its pitfalls and problems, which likely matured into a flexibility which emerged as a virtue of its own.

Woodworking class in a public school

When we consider the cosmopolitan character of this school, we cannot help thinking what a great opportunity the principal and teachers have for instilling in the minds of these men and women from Central Europe the principles of freedom and justice for which Canada stands. The teachers of this school are teaching English to their students, but they are also not losing sight of the broader aim, the Canadianizing of our foreign population.

Toronto Board of Education, Chief Inspector's Report, *Annual Report*, 1928, p.158.

daughter of a Macedonian workman remembers looking at her father's hands during dinner — hands that prodded cattle from a stockyard to abbatoir before cleaning out stock pens. There seems no allowance can be made. Saintliness is measured by the cleanliness of fingernails. A father is condemned.

Mothercraft class at St. Helen's Separate School, 1918

It was demanded that the teacher be a model, an example of Canadian adulthood, whom students could respect and emulate. The teacher was also charged with systematically instructing these foreign students in the ways of the New World, a process which often dismissed the Old World ways as backward, as un-Canadian.

Girls who would once have been instructed in child care by a mother or grandmother now learned mothercraft from teachers or school nurses. Homecare, diet, cooking and, of course, personal hygiene programs stressed a so-called Canadian style home, often at the expense of negative comparison with a student's present home, often advocating new food preparations, housecleaning methods or child care techniques alien to parents or beyond their financial reach.

Even personal hygiene programs could undermine the house. Every morning, for instance, the teacher systematically went up and down the classroom inspecting each student's hands and fingernails for that last trace of dirt which defied the morning wash. A villainous bit of grime would temporarily banish a student to the school sink amid disapproving looks from teacher and schoolmates. As the teacher makes her inspection rounds the

This is the playground of most of the little Jews and Italians of the city. These little ones of the foreign-born constitute one of our greatest social problems. It is important to us that they have opportunity, out in the open, under careful supervision, to fight the influences that come to them from the overcrowding in which their parents persist or are forced into.

The playground is the true melting pot in which all the little foreigners are fused into Canadians. It should, to be effective, be an all-the-year-round-place. It cannot be if all the work has to be done under the blue sky.

In this ward, more than in any other in the city, the children are full of the spirit of play. They have an abandon that is not given to the little ones of the Anglo-Saxon race. Repressed it is easily turned into viciousness. They need the playground even more in short, dark, cold winter days than they do in the brighter ones.

Central Neighbourhood House, Newspaper Clipping Collection Scrapbook

In the Old World, play was a luxury usually reserved for the rich or the very young. There was little room for play when a child became old enough to work or enter a school with a no-nonsense approach to study. Once again the New World was different. Here children were not only encouraged to play, to remain children, but time, parks and playgrounds were set aside specifically for that purpose. Nor was activity confined to specific times or playgrounds. To the dismay of social workers and police, children spilled out of playgrounds into local streets and laneways where adult authority was usually excluded. Often the sound of children at play rang well into the night.

Children were pursued. After-school jobs forced some children to abandon the playground and street while the shadow of an approaching Bar Mitzvah absorbed others in *Chader*. Still other children found their streets periodically patrolled by police and their playgrounds managed by neighbourhood workers who organized games and other activities. Immigrant parents who regarded play as a frivolous waste of time might probably have been bemused if not disparaging to see "English" ladies organizing childrens' activities.

On May 13, 1913, for example, central Neighbourhood House took over the nearby Elizabeth Street playground for a Spring Festival. Fifty children performed for an audience of six hundred adults, "mostly fathers, mothers or relatives who lived in the locality. One group danced the Maypole Dance, another Sir Roger de Coverly and other old fashioned dances, after which the boys took part in a programme of field sports."

But the streets remained the real playground. As one Toronto reporter described an immigrant neighbourhood in 1912, "If the weather is fine, you'll find them in the streets until midnight, or gathered in little groups in corners, alleyways or doorsteps playing with the exuberance peculiar to the little ones of southern and eastern Europe." To social workers this exuberance was a challenge.

Elizabeth Street playground

"Yes then comes the Summertime; but why do you want to know?"

"Because that's the name of that time when you go to that country — not the OLD COUNTRY, but the country where you sleep in a tent and pick flowers and berries and everybody has a little white bed to sleep in — that's the Country that is by that Summertime," she said.

Statistical Report, in St. Christopher House 1:2 (Toronto 1914), p.4.

Summer was always special. Schools closed their doors and hours previously spent at desks in crowded classrooms were made available for play, adventure and, some feared, mischief. For many children, of course, summer meant only a shift from school to factory or from homework to housework. Summer vacation became an economic bonus to some families. Yet even these young labourers usually had weekends free — often to join the systematically organized exodus of children to parks, camps and beaches.

Programs varied. Settlement houses and community organizations operated summer camps for children with four two-week shifts while, at the same time, they received assistance from the Board of Education, the *Toronto Star* Fresh Air Fund and street railway companies to organize day-long excursions out of the city — to Toronto Island, Kew Gardens, Scarboro Bluffs and Port Credit.

Excursion organizers appreciated the importance of their activities; the immigrant child was to learn that Canada extended well beyond the confines of his home, his family and his neighbourhood. Yet, children did not always leave their "foreign" ways at home. A summer teacher at a Board of Education day camp expressed pleasure at the progress of immigrant children but questioned the participation of Jewish children who, it was noted, refused to eat food provided to all children. Maintaining kosher dietary laws, of course, did not diminish with distance from the home kitchen or freshness of the air.

The camps and outings had their effect. The Central Neighbourhood House headworker reported with pride in July, 1914, "'The children have all gained in weight and have had their cheeks painted to a coffee colour by Mother Nature. I feel sure that they will be able to live the next year better on account of their holiday."

Below: Free streetcar rides take children to Sunnyside, 1924

Right: Finnish community summer camp

It is apparent that the government on account of the large immigration we are to receive, must give very close attention to the education of the masses, not only with the view of developing a Canadian spirit, a love for our country and an appreciation of our system of government, but also so far as possible to inoculate our new citizens with the spirit of the empire. The children of our new immigrants, in the natural course of events, may be expected to become good Canadians, but it will require education if they are to appreciate the advantages of imperial unity so patent to most of us who come from British stock.

A.D. McRae, "Canadian Citizenship of the Future," *Proceedings of the Canadian Club of Toronto, 1919-20* (Toronto 1921), p.6.

The foreigner and his children were in Canada to stay. A few might eventually return to the Old Country, but others, many others, would soon come to take their place. The foreigner who remained in Canada long enough could become a naturalized British subject with the same rights as anyone born in Canada. The Canadian-born children of Macedonian, Italian, Pole, Finn or Jew from Russia were already subjects of the crown by birthright.

Nevertheless, many feared that the simple and legal granting of citizenship rights to foreigners after a few years in Canada would lead to abuse. Before a foreigner could even be a Canadian, he, and more particularly his children, must be engendered with feelings of loyalty to Canada, the Empire and the crown, a loyalty marked by respect for the institutions and symbols of nationhood. If this could be achieved, many assumed, the rights of citizenship, including the vote, would lead to responsibility and not abuse. A speaker before the Empire Club in Toronto in 1909 observed, "Today we are making laws for Europeans and other foreigners. In the not very distant future they will begin to make laws for us. This is inevitable, and it seems to me that if we are going to save our country we must inspire these foreigners with our ideals to make them the type of Canadian citizens we want them to be."

Yet, doubts remained whether the foreigner would, or could, transfer loyalty from alien tsars, kaisers, kings and emperors to the British Crown. This made it all the more important to reach the children of foreigners, to ensure that their loyalty to Canada and the crown was not diluted by parental feelings of allegiance to foreign Gods or foreign kings. In both school and organized community activity, national symbols were stressed.

Immigrant children salute their new flag

The older children who came to the House in the afternoon were organized into industrial classes, such as dressmaking, sewing, embroidery and raffia work, and also into self-governing clubs, while the younger ones were entertained with games and stories. In the clubs the children found opportunity for self-expression, and varied and entertaining programmes that they arranged for themselves from time to time.

Annual Report, Central Neighbourhood House, 1915.

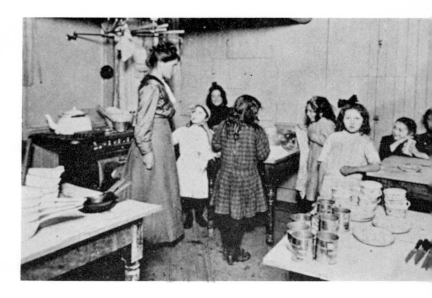

Central Neighbourhood House activities

The 1915 annual report of Central Neighbourhood House points with some pride to the initiative immigrant children took in organizing their own activities "from time to time." It was, however, a guided initiative. The English-speaking workers were always present, always offering assistance, organization and an example to follow. At St. Christopher's House in 1914 five workers lived in residence but, as the annual report pointed out, ongoing settlement work involved additional personnel. "So our added strength comes to us from the North and the South, the East and the West of the city. These friends realize with us that a *real* life is one of co-operation; one must work with and share with these around one, if one is to get the best for one's own life."

Duties of the volunteers varied. In addition to supervising clubs, one might direct a play, another organize a picnic, or tutor in mathematics or teach crafts. Yet, the volunteers' commitment was constrained by distance and the clock. No matter what their duty in the house, the end of the day found them leaving the foreigners' neighbourhood. They returned to neighbourhoods where settlement houses were not required, where the momentary visit of the junkman, the fruit peddler or sewer-cleaning crew was the only foreign intrusion.

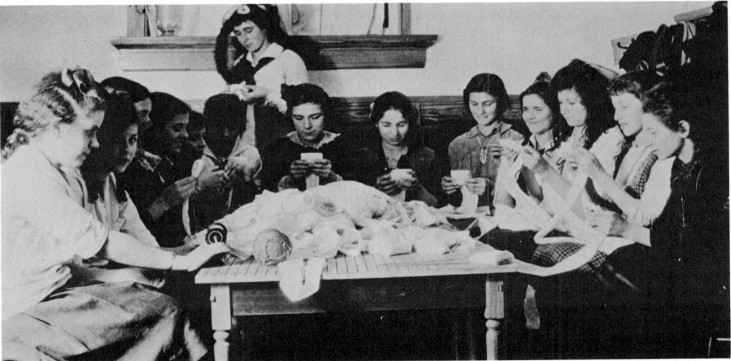

The Pansy Club was in full swing on Saturday afternoon when a Globe reporter visited the Neighbourhood House. A young lady was using copies of magazines and illustrated papers in her efforts at cultivating Canadian nationality in these children of the congested quarter, mostly of foreign parentage and poor circumstances. The girls said they enjoyed the classes as their absorbed interests made evident.

"Settlement Work Has a Good Start," Central Neighbourhood House, Newspaper Clipping Collection Scrapbook.

The *Globe* reporter who visited Central Neighbourhood House during a weekend afternoon recognized that club activities, even of adolescent girls, were geared toward Canadianization. The settlement houses were, as one social worker wishfully described them, "the greatest Canadianizing power that is making for the unifying of all our people into a Canadian race with common aspirations for the future greatness of our country." Questionable grammar, perhaps, but a statement that reflected the underlying passion of the assimilator's campaign.

School and settlement house youth activities were purposefully bound to instill what was commonly labelled as "Principles of Citizenship." The singing of "God Save the King" with fervour by these little Canadians whose parents in many instances had come from all corners of the earth ritually preceded every club meeting. The Jewish immigrant from the Pale might mistrust the trappings of nationalism with an uneasiness tempered in the midst of a pogrom, but his son sits on the executive of the Boy's Imperial Club. The daughter of an Italian road worker welcomed in the city for his "ingenuity, deftness, industry in unskilled labour, and a love of domestic life," becomes treasurer and recording secretary in the Busy Bee

Club. Parents and children cannot help but have different expectations, as they cannot help but have different memories.

Below: Boys' Imperial Club, Roden School, c. 1915

Right: Busy Bee Club, Secord School, c. 1915

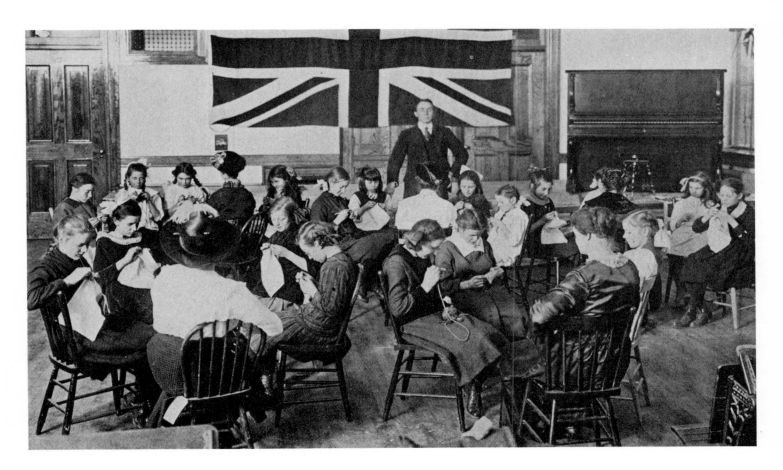

The gang spirit is very strong in the city. Outstanding characters in boy life have no difficulty in keeping a strong body of retainers, ready to back them up in anything they say or do, and, as a rule, faithful in any trouble or dispute in which the gang may be involved. A gang should never be broken up, no matter what offence the members may have committed. It is true that separate units of it might better be weeded out, but never at the risk of breaking up the group. Rather, that gang should be given something that will bind them closer together. The leader is the boy to watch; he will look out for the rest. Give him careful attention, and let him develop to the fullest and best his powers of leadership.

L.W. Tew, "Boy Life in the Ward," in *The Ward Graphic* (1918)

duty of public authority, especially as the freedom offered in Canada could too easily become licence. In 1920 one observer noted, of immigrants, "Liberty is a dangerous intoxicant. . . . The country must assume the duties of parenthood in order to obtain parental respect and devotion."

Children of different backgrounds mingle in the streets

Streets in immigrant neighbourhoods were alive with children. To the social worker who sought to guide these children into organized activities, those children who today preferred the freedom of the street to the structure of school or settlement programs were considered likely to be tomorrow's juvenile delinquents. Indeed a 1918 article in the *Public Health Journal* warned, "we find the largest list of juvenile delinquents among children of immigrants."

In reality, delinquency was not limited to children of immigrants and was usually less pronounced in areas of heavy foreign concentration than in other areas of Toronto. Many police, settlement workers, teachers and public health officials were convinced, nevertheless, that the children of foreigners possessed instinctive and, maybe, primitive traits which, if not properly channelled, would lead to anti-social behaviour. Turning vices into positive virtues was, these assimilationists believed, a

The saloon, the dance hall, the gambling den, the low theatre, and the five cent show, which formerly constituted the only form of relaxation in the dull monotony of the people's lives, give way under the influence of the institutional church to the practical education, intellectual development and social intercourse under uplifting auspices.
Missionary Outlook (Toronto, March 1910), p.58.

Public education was compulsory, but only to age fourteen or sixteen. Even this regulation was conveniently neglected during the labour-short war years. Nevertheless, the children of immigrants and those immigrant young adults who came to Canada too old to fall within the bounds of compulsory school attendance laws were not beyond the concern of educational authorities.

Night schools flourished. Instruction in technical, office and household skills was widely available, but underlining all night school activity was the omnipresent study of English. Special English night classes for the young adult were organized by the Board of Education and settlement houses. As one Toronto social worker explained, the young adult recognizes that eventual success in the New World depends on mastery of English. Accordingly, "he spends all day at hard work, and at night hurries to the evening schools. Naturally, his progress is slow, for while his mind is alert and he is too far advanced for his parents, yet he cannot keep pace with growing youngsters."

Night schools often depended on volunteer teachers or community workers. Although these volunteers were dedicated, few, if any, were trained in the teaching of English as a second language. Often teachers were forced to rely on children's books or improvise with such things as flash cards. In many cases students became frustrated with their own slow progress or the rigidity of classroom study and fell back on learning English as best they could in the street or on the job.

Canadianizing, especially of the hard sell variety was also attempted but with far more limited success. One settlement worker was discouraged to report in 1913 that Italians conspicuously avoided efforts to promote Canadian nationalism. She wrote to her supervisors, "We attempted to give two Italian lectures on Citizenship and failed to draw an attendance either time. In spite of the fact that the lectures were to be given in Italian and that the posters and circulars were printed in Italian. I am sorry to say that we have had to abandon the plan of having Italian lectures. The concerts however promise to be a wonderful success."

Settlement houses and public education authorities were not alone in offering English-language night school classes. Protestant missions to Roman Catholic immigrants and Jews reinforced their proselytizing work with a regular schedule of English classes, many of which predated the settlement house efforts. Presbyterian, Methodist and Baptist programs were, of course, dedicated to saving souls through conversion, but evangelists believed that the would-be convert's resolve could be made stronger if he could but read the Bible in English or participate comfortably in English-language Protestant services.

Right: English lesson at Central Neighbourhood House, c. 1913
Overleaf: Night schools at settlement houses and missions

The Department of Public Health has opened a Mothercraft Class for Italian women in charge of their Italian Nurse, Miss Simoni, this meets at the House once a week and has an average attendance of ten members. A good deal of visiting was done during the month and many people taken to clinics who were reluctant to go or who needed an interpreter when they got there.

Headworkers Report, Central Neighbourhood House, (December 1916).

There is a certain irony in women, many of them mothers several times over, gathering with their youngest children one afternoon a week to learn how to be mothers. Yet, under the careful and caring eye of a public health nurse, groups of immigrant women were introduced to ideas, family practices and concerns which had been either unknown or unnecessary in the Old World.

Italian mothers, who as children had played in the sun all year round but saw their own children in Toronto grow pale during winter months, were introduced to cod liver oil, the importance of warm boots and the handkerchief. What earlier immigrants to Toronto took for granted, the greenhorn had to learn. To ensure an adequate supply of traditional food stuffs during the winter, for instance, new buying and preserving techniques had to be learned, the possibilities of a cold cellar explored and substitutions found for ingredients now suddenly unavailable.

The mothercraft class, however, was not just a simple study group. It was also a social event, an occasion for women with limited opportunity to escape the isolation of housework to gather together. Within the formal class structure they met others who spoke the same language, faced many of the same problems, carried with them the same longing for the old country and, often, expressed the same previously unarticulated uneasiness over life in this new world.

On occasion settlement workers stepped in as intermediaries between the foreign women and a seemingly incomprehensible English Toronto. A settlement worker remembered, "Not so long ago when a City Hall regulation was explained to an Italian and the woman's misinterpretation cleared up with the authorities she explained, 'The Mayor is like God, too high up for us to reach! You are the saints who speak for us!'"

Classes in mothercraft were aimed at all age groups, c. 1913

HEALTH · 904 JAN. 29 1916 [?]N MOTHERCRAFT. 82-84 GERRARD WEST.

138

Babies abound and are the objects of tender solicitation on the part of the nurse.
"Are you feeding the baby just as the doctor told you to?" But the little foreign mother cannot understand. "Me no speak English," she informs the nurse smiling. An interpreter is called in from a neighbouring house and conversation proceeds satisfactorily. The mother insists that her care of the infant is above reproach and that she loves it dearly. Convinced that her words are true, the nurse gives some parting advice about fresh air in the home and leaves with the mother's benediction — "Peace belong to you" — following her.

Central Neighbourhood House, Newspaper Clipping File, 1911.

While doctors generally practised within the confines of an institution, hospital, clinic or school treatment centre, the city's public health nurse took medicine into the streets of Toronto's foreign neighbourhoods. Neatly dressed in a modest suit with a black tie and spotless white blouse, the nurse made daily calls wherever a quarantine patient required inspection, a sick child had been reported, or a change of bandages demanded.

Illness was not new to Jew or Italian, Chinese, Macedonian or Russian immigrant. Children had been born and the sick tended in the old country. Yet, in the New World, in Toronto, traditional methods for treating the sick were not enough. Folk remedies were gradually abandoned or at least combined with the pills, ointment, diet and bed-rest made mandatory by the "English lady." The Jewish mother might well ensure the health of her growing children with the fresh air, good diet and regular milk strongly recommended by the visiting nurse, but just in case she would also take special care that nobody inad-

vertantly stepped over her child thereby stunting growth — just in case.

Although old ways might linger on, the public health nurse made a difference. The nurse's immediacy and her obvious concern, while perhaps not fully understood, was nevertheless appreciated. Miss Young, the nurse who worked with the St. Christopher House community during the First World War years, was welcomed by the settlement and its clientele. The House's annual report for 1914 observes, "the 'calls' are visits, and the 'cases' are our friends and neighbours; and the nurse's work includes all sorts of things that make for cleanliness and health as well as the fight between life and death."

The visiting nurse, 1913

Canada has been the dumping ground for thousands of undesirable immigrants — from the slums of the British cities, from Austria, Poland and other European countries. She is also the victim of colonies of sects who refuse to become assimilated — to become Canadian. This must stop. Our asylums and jails are over full of degenerates, criminals, and mental defectives . . . . Our profession should awaken to the paramount importance of seeing that our fair country is stocked with only the best; and should urge vehemently upon the powers that be the necessity of a thorough inspection of all new-comers.

"Diseased Immigrants," *Canadian Journal of Medicine and Surgery* 46 (September 1919), pp. 278-79.

Members of the medical profession stood in the front rank of those fighting unrestricted immigration into Canada during the years before the depression. Nor was it just the supposed threat of communicable diseases which concerned doctors. Looking after the foreign patients in hospital out-patient departments doctors debated whether or not strange customs and ignorance of health considerations could be hereditary, genetically transmitted from one generation of foreigners to the next.

But if doctors demanded restriction of immigration they also pushed for better public medical facilities for those already in Canada. Toronto General Hospital and the Hospital for Sick Children worked in cooperation with settlement houses and public authorities to establish general health services, milk distribution centres and baby clinics. With care and education, even those "defective" foreigners could give rise to productive offspring. As the *Canadian Lancet* explained in 1908, "Time levels up as well as levelling down. It is a notorious fact that in Australia the descendants of those who were transported as

criminals have made excellent citizens, and rank among the most progressive and well-to-do of that portion of the Empire." Could Canada expect less of its foreign population?

Right: Waiting room, Hospital for Sick Children, 1916

Below: Free milk dispensary, Hospital for Sick Children, 1916

Thousands are being imported annually of Russians, Finns, Italians, Hungarians, Belgians, Scandinavians, etc. The lives and environments of a large number of these have, no doubt, been such as is well calculated to breed degenerates. Who would think of comparing for a moment, in the interests of our country, mentally, morally, physically or commercially, a thousand of these foreigners with a thousand persons of Canadian birth? Practically no effort has been made, no money expended, to secure the best medical and physical development of our boys and girls, while the Government expends over half a million annually for the advancement of improvement of agriculture and stock. Literature is distributed gratuitously advising stock raisers how to properly care for and protect their stock and, in the event of an outbreak of infectious disease, what precautions to take in order to prevent its spread! Surely, then, the child has some right to consideration.

Charles Hastings, "Medical Inspection of Public Schools," *Canadian Journal of Medicine and Surgery* 21 (1907), pp.73-74.

Toronto Public Health Officer Dr. Charles Hastings saw a twofold duty of the school with regard to the health needs of students. In his paper on medical inspection in public schools, originally read before the National Council of Women in Toronto in December 1906, Hastings pointed to the need for both teaching programs designed to acquaint children, especially the children of foreigners, with hygiene and sanitation standards to a "higher order" and regular visits by public health officials to the classroom to ensure the prevention or early treatment of disease.

As Hastings spoke, programs of this type were already well established in the United States. In urban Canada the later arrival of foreign immigrants delayed the introduction of similar schemes in Toronto schools. Before the First World War, however, doctors, dentists, public health nurses routinely visited neighbourhood schools, giving special attention to schools in areas of foreign concentration among whom, it was assumed, disease was more likely.

Public clinics in local hospitals or schools routinely processed those who required care. Sometimes the remedy was more dramatic. In 1904, before regular school inspections began, Dr. Tweedy of the Isolation Hospital examined a Jewish child and discovered diphtheria. The doctor immediatley examined all students in his patient's school. An additional twelve or thirteen cases were discovered. The school was closed.

Below: Free dental clinic in a public school, c. 1911

Right: Emergency admitting at Hospital for Sick Children, c. 1916

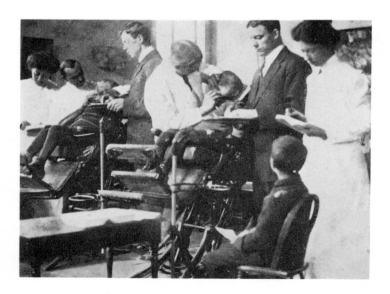

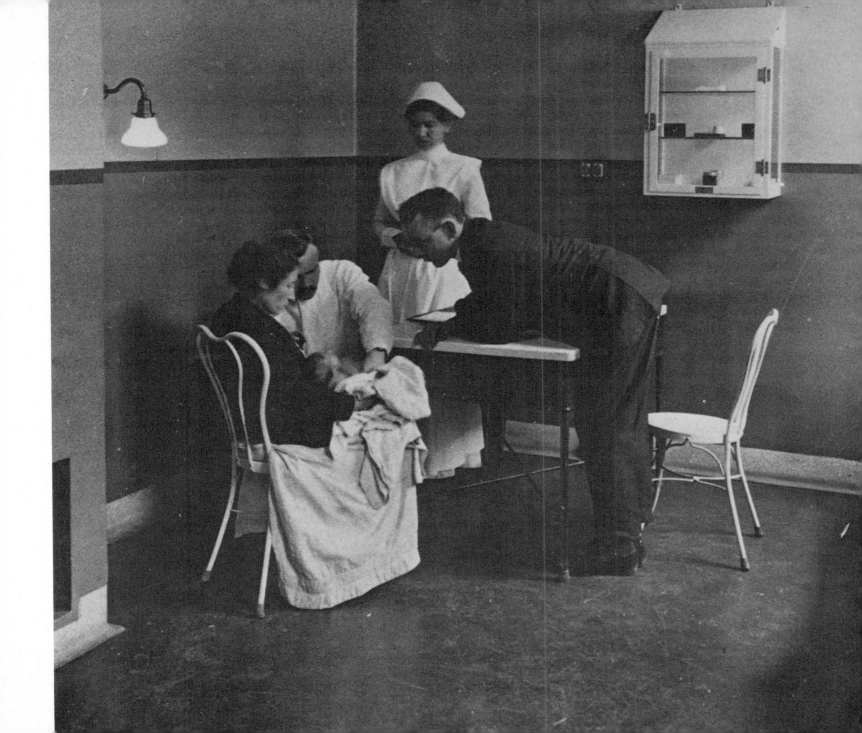

5 RELIGION AND POLITICS

Although the search for decent housing and steady work preoccupied the immigrants, a number of other institutions shaped their Toronto lives and affected the pace of their settling in. Religion had been at the centre of their daily and yearly cycle in the old country, and the Atlantic crossing had affected that too. Even if religious faith survived the sea voyage intact, European church ritual and institutional strength did not. In Toronto, immigrants encountered, often for the first time, religious choice. Whether they had been part of a Jewish minority in a Russian Orthodox society or part of the Christian peasantry of Catholic southern Italy, very few had thought deeply about religious alternatives. In rural Europe, they were what they were, and interdenominational mobility was almost unknown. In Canada, they discovered competing faiths and a setting where the powerful social sanctions against unorthodox religious behaviour that they had known in Europe were greatly attenuated. The thought that religion, like so many other aspects of the European world, might be shucked like an old coat came as a surprise to the immigrants, but it required thinking about.

For example, it was obvious that the English language was the stairway that led to economic success; speaking English was also the first step toward being counted as worth counting by Canadian neighbours and officials. If the new language offered such advantages, how far should one go in mimicking or accepting other Toronto values? If Yiddish, Italian dialect, and Macedonian conversations were to be just secret vices carried on behind closed doors, would not Protestantism be a more practical commitment in Toronto than Judaism or Catholicism?

To varying degrees the act of emigrating itself had been connected with religious survival; so for Jews who had fled Tsarist sabres or Macedonians who had fought pitched battles with Turks or "Patriarchists" (Greeks), the idea of leaving the faith of one's father might be initially unthinkable. On the other hand, the idea that they would someday leave their home had been unthinkable or impious but a short time before. Moreover, the new proselytizers did not wield sabres and scimitars; they offered shelter and participatory togetherness in a lonely new world. Since the decision to leave home, life for the immigrant had become a seemingly endless series of deliberate or hasty adaptations of old ways to new situations. None of them could be certain where the decision to migrate and each choice taken after that might lead. After all, the psychic space involved in changing one's surname and religious affiliation in North America was more than matched by the physical space that had been crossed to get there.

Not surprisingly, the Jews seemed most impervious to the evangelists. Accustomed to being a religious minority and to nurturing their faith in adversity, they had long survived without the support of an institutional church. In that regard, the Ward's relationship to the larger Christian Toronto did not differ from any ghetto in eastern Europe. Folklore, backed by hard reality, provided Jews with countless examples of the family pain, evil consequence, and futility that came when one sought escape from prejudice or oppression through conversion. As the largest group of newcomers and an obvious challenge to the city's Christian homogeneity, the Jews of the Ward were under assault from evangelists. The Presbyterian Mission to the Hebrew People was authorized by that Church's General Assembly in 1907. Faced with the missionary's subtle claim that their effort was not to destroy Judaism but rather fulfill it by preaching Christ as the Messiah, quick establishment of the same familial and traditional networks that had served Jewish survival elsewhere was necessary in the Ward.

It was easy for the newcomer to identify Canada with Protestantism; social agencies and concerned evangelists became confused in the newcomer's limited vision of the legal structure of charity, and native Catholics, usually English-speaking Irish, seemed closer to the Canadian Protestant mainstream that to Italians, Poles, and "Greek Catholics." With the exception of Central Neighbourhood House in the Ward and the Hospital for Sick Children, most social services that the immigrants came in contact with were related to evangelism.

The major Protestant denominations had divided up the newcomers in much the same way as the Great Powers had once divided up the non-European world. Without denying the material good accomplished by the evangelists, one must note that every sect occasionally dropped to the level of military despatches in their missionary literature. Territory occupied; population subdued — that was what counted. The Italian Methodist Mission in the Ward reacted angrily when its best catechist was recruited for mission work in Japan. Was the Ward any less a battlefield against heathenism and moral laxity than Japan? At the same time, the Baptists reached out to the Macedonians and other groups from eastern Europe, sometimes calling their missions Slavic, sometimes Russian. For their work among the Macedonians, they imported a charismatic preacher, John Kolesnikoff, from the mining country of Pennsylvania where he had already had much success. The Presbyterians, as we have seen, directed their missionary activities toward the Jews, and there the identification of Canadianization and Christianization, while it fell short of outright anti-semitism, left some newcomers, particularly the young, with a nagging sense of otherness that was not simply the feeling of being immigrant nor the same as pride in being chosen. Methodists concentrated their effort on the Italians and Chinese. Work among the latter, of course, was connected with the missions in Asia; the former was a new battleground, taking the attack to the very heart of an old enemy, the Roman Catholic Church. In turn, the Catholic Church, dominated by the Irish and lacking in lay initiative, was slow to notice the "great activity of non-Catholics among the immigrants"; it was some time before the Church, "whose adherents are counted by the hundreds of thousands amongst the foreign element now seeking our shores," counter-attacked. In many ways, the immigrants were the foot soldiers and non-combatants in this confused crusade, and although dedicated workers and clergy of every religion thought first of the material well-being of the immigrants, there were casualties.

Giving up the religion of one's forefathers was not a price that the immigrant should have had to pay and not all native Canadians wished to exact that price. There was innocence as well as prejudice in the evangelists' desire to uplift the newcomers and to welcome them into the mainstream of Toronto life. The camaraderie of the Italian Methodist missions in the Ward and then in the Manning-Henderson or Dufferin-Brandon areas are remembered by Catholic and Protestant Italians alike. One need only glance at the photographs of the Macedonian or Russian Baptist brass bands to sense the fellow feeling of the groups. Yet, the implication — left by teachers, evangelists and most social workers — that maybe being Protestant was part of being Canadian was an acid that ate away at the relationship between an immigrant and his heritage and very often between an immigrant and his children as well. The sudden confrontation with an array of religious beliefs led the young to secularism and an unwillingness to follow old rituals. Sometimes, in their efforts not to appear as greenhorns, they discarded their religious culture too carelessly.

Passing over to a "modern" denomination was the obvious way of completing the psychological trip from a rural or a small-town environment to the New World city and modernity. In fact, though, no one was really able to practise the faith of his fathers as it had been practised in Europe. The changes were subtle and probably could barely be observed by outsiders, but things that had been natural ritual in the old country had to be purposeful ideology in the new one or they would cease to exist, and ritual, like every other aspect of folk culture, was a living thing that borrowed from the environment and the changing frame of mind. A mass and procession on the feast day of Saint Rocco looked "very Italian" to native Torontonians, but an Italian immigrant saw only the strange compromises made by those who had left their *paese*. The priest who celebrated the mass was Irish; a Jewish boy was the solo trumpeter and the D'Angelo band closed the service with a rendition of "God Save the King." At best it was a parody of the pomp and intensity of the same feast as it was held in many Italian villages. At the same time, distinctions in the Jewish community between the orthodox and the reformed increasingly reflected the impact of the American environment as much as the *Haskala* (Jewish Enlightenment).

For the eastern orthodox Christians who came to the city, religious practice changed as well. In North America, they could self-consciously identify their church with ethnic survival in a manner that would have been unsafe in the old country. Ruthenians, Bukovinians and Galicians could work to create independent churches, free of the interference of Tsar or Austrian Emperor. They could also try to free themselves from entanglement with patriarchs, exarchs and popes that they did not trust. Just as the Baptists looked to the earlier Macedonian immigration to the Pennsylvania mines for their proselytizer, the Orthodox Macedonians, gathering together in Stoyanoff's and Velianoff's bakery on King Street in 1910, agreed to tithe one another a certain amount per village of origin in order to send to Pennsylvania for a priest. In these ventures, the newcomers showed a degree of lay initiative in religious affairs that had not been necessary in the homeland but that equalled that of their Protestant Canadian contemporaries. Men reared in a village church created an urban church embracing parishoners from many villages. No matter how traditional the architecture or how much Canadians might see the immigrant's religion as a survival from rural Europe, the newcomers knew that was only partly true. It was an adaptation to the environment. Linked as it was with the seasons, topography, and moods of the homeland, ritual could not be transplanted unscathed. The older folks among the immigrants found the little changes in sacramentals, liturgy and religious habits to be nagging reminders of uprootedness and of the traditions that had almost been sacrificed.

For those who had made the adjustment, though, the ethnic churches helped to define who one was in North America. Very often the associations in and around the church brought people a larger sense of nationality than they had ever had in the narrowly circumscribed society they had left behind. Paradoxically, growth of national feeling came after one came to North America. Church-sponsored after-school language and culture classes and mutual aid societies fostered a larger and more ideological sense of fellow feeling.

Some groups were fortunate in their national cohesion. The Poles in the city, who organized a Sons of Poland Association by 1907, had no church of their own before 1911. They worshipped together in a chapel at the city's Roman Catholic Cathedral. Eugene O'Keefe, brewer, banker, and philanthropist, saw the Poles going to mass from the chancery window one Sunday morning, and, moved by their piety and their desire for rites in their own tongue, O'Keefe bought a large unused Presbyterian church for them. That church became St. Stanislaus Parish, for many years the central religious and cultural institution of the Poles. Nonetheless, national loyalties and identities among the immigrants, like religious ties themselves, were in flux. The Sons of Poland Association, for example — on the ground that the Kings of Poland had reigned over much of east central Europe — welcomed Lithuanians and Ruthenians as members. At the same time, the small group of Lithuanians in the city, too few in number to have their own parish, did form a separate St. Joseph's Lithuanian Society. If one remembers that neither Polish nor Lithuanian immigrants had left an independent nation behind them and that attempts to Russify the

one or Polonize the other had gone on for a century, the strength and the persistence of ethnicity becomes apparent.

So the growth of ethnic parishes and national churches, while they preserved and transplanted much of the culture of the old country, also subtly changed the immigrants. At Our Lady of Mt. Carmel, Barese, Sicilian and Venetian patron saints rubbed shoulders in a way that they would not have in Italy. At St. Stanislaus Church, people from Kielce, Galicia and western Poland were all for the moment simply Poles, happy enough to hear a sermon delivered with any regional accent. Macedonians, although they organized brotherhoods based on single villages, came together to create St. Cyril and Methody Church which they shared with Bulgarians but not with fellow villagers who were "Patriarchists" (i.e., supporters of the Greek Orthodox Patriarch). In all instances, local identity—the *paese*, the *spiti*, the *shtetl*, the village—gave way to identities such as Italian, Pole, Greek that had been secondary or latent at home. The national labels used so loosely by Canadian society added to this enlarged group feeling. Men who would have answered to anyone that they were Bialystoker or Litvak, Napolitano or Friulan, from Lerin or Zhelevo, sized up the interrogator, measured his probable ignorance of European geography and answered Jew, Italian, or Macedonian. It was not that local loyalties and distinctions from the old country ceased to be important, but rather that the immigrants faced a new and larger social and political reality.

The relationship of religion to national feeling, the growing sense of group that came in the face of prejudice, but also from nostalgia and mobility, had important consequences for the immigrant in the New World. It meant that few people could escape the labelling that went on from within and without immigrant society. It meant that a pattern of group behaviour came into existence, even if there were constant and instructive exceptions. Ethnicity affected the immigrant's relationship to politics of both the Europe he had abandoned and the Toronto that he needed to survive in. Many had barely left the Old World behind when its political upheavals seem to pursue and challenge them.

No matter how economic the motivation to migrate had been, politics or hostility to central governments had figured in the decisions men made in coming to North America. Toronto had an array of people who welcomed the collapse of the oppressive eastern empires, particularly the Tsarist regime. Jews, Poles, Finns, Lithuanians, Ukrainians, Slovaks, Czechs, Croats, Syrians and Armenians— all had reason to rejoice at the beginnings of the "final war for freedom." Among immigrants of these groups, national feeling ran high; some felt that they were the only representatives of their people free to speak out or act. The participation of Toronto's immigrants in the First World War reflected the ambivalence of their loyalties, but it helped to win their acceptance in Canadian society. Without armies of their own, Jews, Macedonians and Ukrainians volunteered to serve in the Canadian army. Other Jews fought in the Jewish Legion. For them, Zionism, their brothers in the Russian Pale and loyalty to England were all worthwhile causes. Obviously, there were moments of discomfort as alliances produced strange bedfellows; Jews were more at ease with the Russian ally after the fall of the hated Tsar, and for none of the immigrants was there that naïve and clear duty to Empire and freedom that pervaded old-stock Canadian rhetoric. Being immigrant was a confused status and that led to confused loyalties in time of war. Macedonians joined a war effort in which one of the enemies was the Bulgarian state, traditional champion of their national rights, yet they hoped a free Macedonia would rise from the ashes. Galicians, Ruthenians and Bukovinians fought against the Central Powers, and yet

German victory might have been the only hope for a free Ukraine. At war's outbreak, startled immigrants had to report to the Office of the Registrar for Alien Enemies on Adelaide Street in Toronto. After all, they had entered the country as subjects of the Austrian Emperor. Croats had to be registered because they were Austrian subjects; Syrian Christians were listed as Turks. The very oppression that had caused men to flee complicated their existence in North America. The Sons of Poland worked to clear men from the city who were interned as enemy aliens so that they could fight for Free Poland; it is not inconceivable that a man considered a Ruthenian loyal to the Austrian Emperor one day was a Polish Nationalist ally of the British Empire the next.

The First World War had its most interesting impact on the Italians in the city. At the outset of the war, Italy was a member of the Triple Alliance and thus an enemy of the British Empire. Social workers reported that there was more feeling than usual against Italian workers and many were being laid off. By 1915, Italy had done a diplomatic about-face and joined Great Britain and France against the Central Powers. There was great enthusiasm among Italians in Canada, and Canadian support for the Italian war effort manifested itself in the raising of $60,000 in one day for the Italian Red Cross.

If the First World War pointed up the uncertainty and the contradictions of immigrant loyalties in a dramatic way, the newcomers fluctuated between interest in Canadian politics and concern with the fate of the old country. This was most obvious in the development of trade union activism. A high percentage of the newcomers, particularly those involved in contract and seasonal work, found little opportunity to develop union politics, but it was different in the needle trades. It was among the militant cloakmakers and other immigrant work groups that not just unionism but politics of the left emerged; men overcame ethnic hostilities to work for common goals of social justice. The same question that had worried Jewish workers and intellectuals in the Pale of Settlement — to stay in Jewish Bundist movements or to join the Polish socialists or the Russian social revolutionaries — reappeared in the Spadina area of Toronto. In the Eaton's strike of 1912, unionism won out over ethnicity, and Jew and Gentile operatives worked together against the company.

More typically, though, the immigrant worker had to fall back on the narrowest circle of his own kind. The combination of the economic need for protection against catastrophe and the increasing awareness that their very identity was threatened in the new setting brought men together in immigrant societies and clubs.

Every group who came to the city showed remarkable initiative in these efforts to guard against fate and the hostile environment. *Tongs* among the Chinese, *landsmanshaft* burial societies, *mutuo soccorso* (mutual aid societies) and village clubs among Italians and Macedonians were the best defence against solitude; they were the only social insurance available. The societies dealt with the dead, the maimed, and forgotten. Men dreaded being buried in a strange land in a strange way. In every immigrant's childhood there had been stories of earlier men from the village who had crossed the sea and vanished without a trace. Their families lived in limbo. The societies themselves were born in grim and more practical circumstances, but with the growth of unionism, occupational diversity, and improving safety conditions on the job, some of the Benevolent Societies grew into patriotic, social or political clubs. The Umberto Primo Benevolent Society asked the city to fly the colours on Garibaldi's name day and Macedonian societies gathered to commemorate the Ilinden rising; such patriotism had grown in exile.

Slowly from these neighbourhood or job-based organizations there emerged men with political clout. It seems improper to characterize these men as immigrant politicians or to see their politics as a variety of the ward-heeling that went on in larger immigrant concentrations in cities like New York or Chicago. While labour union activities had drawn some men into Canadian politics before they were comfortable with the English language and had a degree of security and leisure, that was premature. Most immigrants needed time to develop the confidence and the free time to become involved in politics, and very often when they found such opportunity they continued to be as interested in the politics of their homeland as they were in Canadian or Toronto government. To rise in the Conservative or the Liberal parties required a more obvious process of assimilation or integration than did union politics. Sometimes older settlers from the same areas of Europe as the newcomers became their leaders; sometimes *prominenti* or *balebatisheh yidn* arose among the newcomers and saw political prominence as the logical consequence of their social or economic success. But it was not until the 1920s that the newcomers became significant in politics, and even then bloc voting and "ethnic politics" did not really exist in Toronto.

152

The value of the street meeting is apparent from the following incident: — Several years ago Brother Kolesnikoff sent one of his religious tracts to Macedonia, which fell into the hands of a number of people, who through it were led to accept the truth and to see their duty in regard to baptism. Ten families of these enlightened Macedonians worshipped together and were known as Baptists, although they had not been baptized because there was no Baptist minister in that district. From this company of believers in Macedonia, three men came to Canada. They were employed by the C.P.R. on construction work, and for a time their boarding-car was sidetracked in Toronto at the foot of Trinity Street. One Sunday the men heard the Macedonian band from their car and inquired who were these street preachers. Being told they were Baptists, the three Macedonians became deeply interested and at once sought the meeting. Inquiring who the leader was, they learned it was Kolesnikoff—a name that raised their interest to white heat, for he was the author of the tract that had been the means of bringing joy to their lives, and of directing their feet in the path of obedience. The street-meeting dismissed, the workers introduced themselves to the missionary and told him their story of the movement in Macedonia that was initiated by means of this tract. They thanked God for bringing them to Toronto, for now they found one who could baptize them.

C.J. Cameron, *Foreigners or Canadians* (Toronto 1913), p.66.

Even before the establishment of a Macedono-Bulgarian Orthodox parish in Toronto, the Baptists had shown interest in proselytizing Macedonian bachelor nav-vies in the King Street–Eastern Avenue area. The Canadian Baptists found a preacher named John Kolesnikoff, a "man sent from God," in the words of one pamphlet, who had had great success among Macedonian labourers and miners in the Pennsylvania anthracite fields. Kolesnikoff came to Toronto in the summer of 1908 to do a study of the missionary possibilities among the Macedonians and other Slavs in the city. He reported that he had visited over 450 Macedonians and Bulgarians in the east end and that he had discovered almost that many Ruthenians in the Ward and central districts of the city.

Within a few years there were Baptist missions for Slavs throughout the city. On King Street East, a mission hall served "Bulgarians, Macedonians, Servians and Montenegrins, Turks and Greeks." Missions on Elizabeth Street and on Dundas Street in West Toronto served Russians, Ruthenians and Poles. Kolesnikoff was the moving spirit behind all of this effort, organizing brass bands, picnics, street meetings. Mission halls served as labour exchanges as well as "bible depositories." The Baptists reckoned that their work affected about 75 per cent of the newcomers; their rate of conversion was quite low and such estimates were often made to encourage continuing support from the larger church bodies rather than as sober reflections of reality. Yet the Macedonian Baptists provided an avenue to rapid assimilation and occasionally dramatic and public conversions such as the ones described above. The crypto-Baptist navvies were led to Jarvis Street Baptist Church to be born again.

Far right: Rev. John Kolesnikoff, Macedonian Baptist preacher, c. 1912
Right: King Street Russian Mission brass band

Let them give us a Ruthenian bishop, some priests, be they English or French, Basilians or Redemptorists, some priests who will pass over to the Ruthenian Rite until they can have priests of their own, and let me add, a paper and some pecuniary assistance and 95% of those people will be saved. What a formidable force against Protestant invasion.

Letter from the President of the Catholic Church Extension Society to Archbishop McEvay of Toronto, (October 23, 1909).

The Catholic Church Extension Society believed, or at least professed, that Catholic and Uniate immigrants were seduced away from the Church by a clever Protestant campaign that included approximating as closely as possible the rituals of the Catholic Church. There was an Independent Church established among the Ruthenians, for example, which had mass, the confessional, the seven sacraments, pictures and images of the Virgin, etcetera. But, in fact, the evangelists reached the newcomers by honest effort and warmth, not artifice. They provided the human scale that the immigrant recalled in his village church and that he sensed the lack of almost immediately upon entering the larger urban parishes of the city. Writing from Buffalo, Father Leo Sembratowicz, a graduate of the Ruthenian Pontifical College and a nephew of a former Uniate Metropolitan of Lemberg in Galicia, tried to explain to the diocesan leaders in Toronto why they could not easily control their Slavic flock. Father Sembratowicz had visited the Ruthenians in West Toronto and found their spiritual life at low ebb. Among the problems they faced was the absence of their own clergy. French Oblates tried to serve them but had not learned the language well enough to handle confessions. Basilian monks had come to Canada but they were neither as educated nor esteemed by the immigrants as the old parish clergy had been. The monks had been chosen because of the Latin Rite's prejudice against married clergy, but, according to Father Sembratowicz, only married secular clergy from Galicia could restore a sense of community and participation to the immigrants.

Right: Russian Baptist Mission on Elizabeth Street, 1912

Below: Christmas dinner at the King Street Baptist Mission, 1909

The Missionary influence in the Ward has reached a high pitch among the Jewish children. The missionaries conduct sewing schools and Sunday schools, in order to attract the Jewish children, and at the same time accustom them to singing Christian hymns.

Canadian Jewish Times, quoted by Rev. S. Rohold, "Israel's Religious Condition and the Church Duty" in *Address to the Pre-Assembly Congress of the Presbyterian Church* (Toronto, 1913) pp. 143-44.

As early as 1898, the City Council received a petition from Jews in the community that steps be taken "to prohibit attacks being made on the Jewish religion by a person who discourses on the subject on the public streets of the city." The favourite device of a renegade Jew, H. Singer, was to intercept groups of Jews in the Ward on the sabbath and harangue them about their religious obstinacy and wrongheadedness.

As the numbers of Jews in the city increased, the attempts to convert them took on more institutional and more subtle guises. The presence of two synagogues "within three minutes walk of Massey Hall" and the fact that the two *shuls* had formerly been evangelical churches aroused a combination of animosity and proselytizing determination among the Presbyterians particularly. A mission with financial support from the latter church was opened on Terauley Street in 1908. S.B. Rohold, a converted Palestinian Jew, was the head of the mission. Gospel services existed side by side with sewing classes. "Each evening a school for men for the study of the English language is held. This is a fixed feature of the work and continues throughout the year. As soon as a Jew is able to read the Bible becomes the textbook." Other efforts were made after that of Rohold. In 1914, a newly built mission known as the Christian Synagogue came into existence at 165 Elizabeth Street in the heart of the Ward.

158

The moral character of the Greek Church people is not nearly as low as one might infer from writers in the press. True, the sin of lying in every-day affairs is somewhat prevalent, but the oath is to them most sacred. The type of manhood developed by this Church is decidedly better than that of the Romish Church from the same land and among people of the same educational advantages.

C.H. Lawford, "About the Foreigners," *The Missionary Outlook* (July 1905), p.148.

A large Slavic community grew up around the Toronto Junction and in the areas where Dundas West intersected with the main east-west arteries. The church in the picture opposite was described in the city directory as a Russian Orthodox Church. Nearby was a Ukrainian Baptist Mission. As we have seen, Catholic authorities referred to those in communion with Rome as Ruthenians, an ethnic designation, as often as they used the word Uniate, a religious designation. The Orthodox had even more difficulty than the "Greek Catholics," or Uniates, in providing clergy and organizing parishes. As a state church in Tsarist Russia, they had depended on the government for much of their organizational structures and initiative.

Ukrainians had to depend on the Tsarist-sponsored Russian Orthodox Church of North America, a church which at first had more Aleuts and Eskimoes in it than Europeans. After 1902, a further split occurred and the beginnings of a truly autochonous North American Church began. In 1913 a Greek Catholic Church came into being in Canada to fight defections to Protestantism, Roman Catholicism, and orthodoxy. This Church, led by Bishop Budka, often adhered too closely to Austrian government policy and Roman Catholic leadership to satisfy the Ukrainian immigrants in Canada. The problem of na-tional and religious identity became an evolving historical situation as often as not dependent on the skills and honesty of clergy in a very local situation. Ruthenian, Galician, Bukovinian, Ukrainian on the one hand, Russian Orthodox, Greek Orthodox, Greek Catholic, Uniate, Independent Greek Church (Presbyterian) were religious adjectives and ethnic labels that flowed through the immigrant communities from the Austrian and Russian Empires. These confusions merely reflected the difficulties involved in re-establishing ancestral ritual and ways of worship in the new North American conditions.

Russian Orthodox Church on Royce Avenue, 1923

Dedication of Parish Hall, Sts. Cyril and Methody Church

We the Macedono-Bulgarians, residing in Toronto, Canada, having involuntarily left our fatherland due to oppression and persecution, but, who are however true to our race, language, church and traditions, united around our national church, Sts. Cyril and Methody, have decided to build this parish hall to serve as a meeting place from which we can derive learning and moral benefit, and wherein our children will be acquainted with one another in order to curtail their dispersion into the various ends of this large city, and to get together from time to time in their own place and to know that they are from one race, and that they have one common national ideal, even though in Canada, and which they should not forget. A Macedono-Bulgarian can be a worthy citizen of Canada and at the same time may be a true son of his fatherland, and his freedom, prosperity, and good fortune may do great things so long as this wish is entertained in his heart.

50th Anniversary Jubilee Almanac of the Macedonian Bulgarian Orthodox Cathedrals Sts. Cyril and Methody, pp.54-55.

Just as the Baptists had found their preacher to the Macedonians working among the immigrants in Pennsylvania, the men who banded together to create the first Macedono-Bulgarian Orthodox parish in the city found their priest, the Hieromonak, later Archimandrite, Theophilact. He had been sent out by the Bulgarian exarch and had already founded several parishes in Pennsylvania. He became the parish priest of St. Cyril and Methody Church in Toronto. The church was built with funds raised by the immigrants who had an elaborate system of tithing by village of origin. In 1911, the Russian Metropolitan Platon of New York, assisted by Father Theophilact and other church dignitaries, dedicated the new church.

The parish prospered and was at the same time the religious and the national centre of Macedonian life in Toronto. Thwarted in their efforts toward national independence in the Balkans, Macedonians depended upon the economic success and the nationalist fervour of those in North America to keep alive the hopes for a free country. At the same time, it was important that the immigrants in North America remained close to one another socially and culturally. So a committee met to discuss the building of a parish hall. The dedication of that Hall when it was built included the eloquent statement of concern for both Canada and the old country quoted above. No more honest nor moving statement for the right to plural loyalties could be made.

Right: Dedication of the community centre of Saints Cyril and Methody Macedonian Orthodox Church, 1927

Below: Metropolitan Platon dedicating the first Macedonian Orthodox Church in Toronto, 1911

162

The Italian population is constantly changing and while at times, it seems discouraging, the changes are in the end beneficial, because those who have been converted in our Mission return to Italy and to other Italian colonies and preach the Gospel to their own countrymen.

Toronto Italian Mission, *Annual Report 1907*, p.75.

As in the case of the Macedonians, the Protestant churches were first to reach out to the Italian immigrants who had begun to settle in the city. Methodist ministers and catechists, many of them Italian, worked in the Ward at the Little Flower Mission and elsewhere to convert and serve the Italians. Italians in Toronto had been unable to convince the Roman Catholic diocese of the need for a national parish, even when the relative success of the Methodists was apparent. Some men took advantage of the visit of the Apostolic Delegate, the diplomatic agent of the Pope and an Italian, to present a petition asking that an Italian priest be found to serve the growing community. The Delegate sent a Rev. Pietro Pisani to Toronto to minister to the Italian colony there and to prepare a report on the number and condition of the Italian faithful in the community. Shortly after that, Our Lady of Mt. Carmel parish, on the western edge of the Ward, became the centre of Italian religious life in the city. There was always difficulty in getting good secular clergy to come from Europe, particularly Italy, and the first Italian priest who came to the Ward was found to have forged papers and the hint of scandal about him. The successors to that first priest worked hard and religiously for their flock but had little relationship with the larger diocesan structure. There is no question but that those Italians who became involved with the Methodist efforts were drawn more quickly into

the processes of assimilation. The Mission's sewing and English classes were larger than its religious services, and one of the directors, the Rev. Taglialatela, betrayed the unconscious process of Canadianizing when he commented that "the best Italian families living here are those who came some time ago — although they were, at that time, worse than the worst of today."

Catholic and Protestant Italian religious life

By what process shall we Canadianize the foreign immigrant? The public school, the press, social intercourse, labor organizations and political institutions are all doing much to destroy national prejudices, to break down language barriers that separate the various colonies of foreigners from one another and from the native population, to impart to all newcomers the knowledge of the English tongue, and to reduce the mixed mass to a homogeneous people. But serviceable as these agencies are for certain ends, they fail to touch the inmost springs of the soul, to unfold the noblest qualities of character, or to promote a true unity of ideal and of like. There is but one all sufficient method by which this goal is reached; we shall Canadianize the foreigner by Christianizing him.

C.J. Cameron, *Foreigners or Canadians?* (Toronto 1913), p.16.

In Canada, immigrant languages were often in danger of becoming only family dialects, understood by a limited circle of relatives and fellow-townsmen. Often the immigrant's daily language had approached that status even before he made the journey across the Atlantic, but in the old country there had been schoolteachers, officials and intellectuals who spoke some higher version of his dialect. The desire to maintain social solidarity became intertwined with efforts to promote the written language of the homeland and to keep the Canadian-born offspring of immigrants aware of their national heritage. That last— national heritage— was in some instances a new consideration, as we have seen. The struggle between Yiddishists and Hebraicists among the Jews, between Zionists and those concerned with their place in Canada was parallelled in most groups. Should the Greek national past be taught in the church by priests or was there a separate and secular patriotic tradition and literary language that should be taught by laymen? Did the creation of a branch of the Dante Alighieri Society, headed by a Canadian professor and sponsored by the Central Neighbourhood House signal the survival of Italian culture among the immigrants or the ideological efforts of the Italian Foreign Ministry and some Italianate social workers to bring the immigrant navvies, mostly southerners, into conformity with Italian official nationalism?

Right: Greek language and culture class at St. George's Greek Orthodox Church, Bond Street, c. 1920

But hard 'tis the trumpet fierce calling afar,
Its summon is rousing the valleys to war.
The banners are floating o'er mountain and sea,
With golden words gleaming and crest of the free
And brave Garibaldi rides forth in his might
And Victor Emmanuel leads far in the fight . . . .

W.A. Sherwood, "The Italian Fruit Vendor," in *The Canadian Magazine* (November 1895), p.60.

For a bittersweet moment in 1915, the gap between the image of Garibaldi, liberal hero of the Risorgimento, and the uneducated and unwelcome Italian navvies in Canada seemed to close. They were made of the same stuff as Garibaldi, Victor Emmanuel II, and the romantic heroes of English schoolboy readings. Italian immigrants throughout Canada responded to the national call to arms to defend Italy from the hated *Tedeschi* (Austrians). Many of them were still in the *riserva* and subject to military call up. The British government had an agreement with its allies that it would expedite the return of reservists who were immigrants or travellers anywhere in the Empire. High Italian migration to Canada occurred in the years 1913, 1914, and there was a natural correlation between how recently one had arrived in Canada and how likely one would be to still be a reservist or to be vitally interested in the homeland's welfare. A train left Vancouver bound for Montreal picking up volunteers and reservists along the way. It was met by enthusiasts and brass bands when it arrived in Toronto. The slogans on the train cars reflected the ambivalence of their enthusiasm. Old Italian Irredentist themes such as, "We go to free Trent and Trieste," hung side by side with "Britons, we are here," and more simply, "Andiamo a fare la guerra" (We go to make war).

Very shortly after the trains bearing the Italian men had left Toronto, certain realities were brought home to the small groups of dependents who had remained behind. No provision had been made for any systematic support or welfare for women who had lost their men to the war effort. Memorials were festooned with Italian tricolor flags and pictures of Bersaglieri appeared on magazine and pamphlet covers, but the truth was that the dependents of those Macedonians, Jews and others who had volunteered for the Canadian army faced less financial hardship and uncertainty than the Italian families; whose men had, after all, gone off to serve a foreign army.

Above right: Italian reservists marching off to war, Yonge and Dundas, 1915

Below: Mayor Tommy Church and Italian reservists at a rally in support of the war effort, 1915

Below right: Italian reservists gathering in Toronto, 1915

Now it is different —we know —(you and I) — that the Belgians, Serbians, the Italians, the Russians and their comrades are closely allied with us in the common struggle for freedom and are even now fighting and dying side by side with our relatives and friends — for humanity — for us. What about these "Foreigners" in our midst? Shall we reciprocate the help they have given in Europe by helping them here? Shall we (you and I) the custodians of Canada's honor show them that we have an interest in their welfare?

The Ward Graphic (Central Nieghbourhood House, 1918), p.1

When an immigrant volunteered for service in the First World War, his motives may have ranged from concern for his homeland or a Canadian sense of duty to the Empire on the one hand, to a belief in the struggle for democracy on the other. In one respect the motive did not matter; immigrants could sense a perceptible increase of "respectability" in the eyes of their Canadian neighbours. Somehow their personal qualities mattered less than the comportment of their mother country. If they had emigrated from a land allied to the British, they themselves were allies, even though the act of emigration may have been a declaration of personal war on the empire they fled. If they had emigrated from one of the Central Powers, few people were willing to trust them.

The war years, although national passions brought from Europe were often revived, were years of rapid assimilation. Young men who left Macedonian or Jewish homes to serve in the Canadian army naturally acculturated more quickly than they would have under parental or neighbourhood supervision. At the same time, those who remained behind found a great variety of new job opportunities in the city. That was, of course, partly because so many working-age men had gone to war but also because of the wave of sympathy for those countries and peoples who were allies of the British Empire.

Below: Canadian member of the Jewish Legion before embarkation to the Palestine front, 1915

Right: Macedonian volunteers to the Canadian army, 1916

170

Then there was the tripping, care-free march of the victorious legions of Dombrowski: "Jeszce Polska Nie Zgrinela" (All is Not Yet Over With Poland) welling up in their merriest moments, as when in great cheering train-loads they began their long journey to France —and to Poland. But from the very depths of hearts saddened with the suffering of their beloved land came the solemn, stately "Boze Cos Polske" (O God, Protector of Poland), by common consent regarded in Niagara Camp as the National Hymn of Poland. Men and women who have heard all that is most impressive in music have often stood with tear-filled eyes as thousands of Poles poured forth in this sublime hymn the pent-up emotion of a hundred and fifty years of persecution.

J.M. Gibbon, "The Foreign Born," *Queen's Quarterly* (April-June 1920), p.346.

Raising men and money for the war effort was important to all the allies who had emigrants in North America. In some cases, North America itself was the cradle of nation-states as yet unborn. Czechs, Poles and Yugoslavs used North America as their behind-the-lines reservoirs of money, manpower and hope. Serbia's heroic defence against the German juggernaut had won much sympathy in England and America, and Serbian military delegations were welcomed as recruiters in the United States and in Canada. Recruiters worked through notables in the local immigrant community to raise men and money.

The Poles were the best organized of those peoples who had no government to represent them. No one doubted their national existence as a people or their value as a counterweight to Wilhelmian Germany and perhaps to Russia as well. Polish authorities were given permission to set up a military training camp in the Niagara Peninsula and Polish volunteers from the United States were trained there. St. Stanislaus parish in Toronto, closely linked through its clergy with the American Poles, took an active part, sending volunteers, money, and a chaplain.

Below: Members of the Serbian War Mission in Toronto, c. 1916

Right: Polish volunteers

Is Eaton's a Sweat Shop?
The Jewish operators are to be congratulated on the stand they have taken on this question. In order to protect 65 Gentile operators who were in imminent danger of losing their positions, they stood behind them and are still standing behind them today. Would any organization of Gentile operators do as much for the Jews?

Jack Canuck (February 24, 1912), p.8

In a world where neither government nor business willingly protected the industrial worker, the immigrants had to protect themselves from the unexpected. Having fled Tsarist oppression and local violence by employers in Europe, the man or woman who came to Toronto was determined to guard his family against catastrophe — the kind of catastrophe that followed the loss of an arm to a shearing machine or a capricious change of work rules and security by an employer. Many of the Jewish workers in the garment industry were aware of the employers' counter-attacks that had come after 1905 in the Pale. Consortia of employers had tried to reduce wages by 35 to 40 per cent and to abolish artisan traditions of job tenure. In Toronto the introduction of piecework, speed-ups and sub-contracting seemed to threaten the worker and his family in the same way. The only answer was union shops and strike action. The roots of militance lay less in the traditions of the Jewish Bund or the Finnish Social Democrats and more in the immigrant reality. One's own kind had to provide help in adversity; no one else would. The new unionism was strongly laced with old fellow feeling and locals composed of only one immigrant group were common.

In the unions, ethnic identity could be maintained without playing into the hands of those who habitually tried to play off one group against another. Only unions could defeat those who saw immigration and immigrants as the chief means of maintaining a low-paid and docile work force.

For example, the pages of the *Labour Gazette* abound with attempts at organization or strikes by Italian navvies in the backland or as close to the city as South Parkdale in 1911. In almost every case the workers were forced back to work at the same or reduced wages. In isolation and without the support of a nearby ethnic community, the railroad navvy striker could be dismissed or driven back by police or GTR and CPR security forces into their bunkcars and submission. Only the garment district provided the class setting for confrontation between the industrial worker and the employer. Ironically ethnic and artisan values figured in the struggle more than any nascent proletarian consciousness.

Bottom right: A share in the Labour Lyceum, a centre of Jewish union activity on Spadina Avenue

Top right: Toronto Cloakworkers' Union, 1911

The Toronto Labor Lyceum Association, Limited

NUMBER 4084 SHARES One

This Certifies that Mr. F. Wallerstein is the owner of One Shares of the Capital Stock of

The Toronto Labor Lyceum Association, Limited

transferable only on the books of this Corporation in person or by Attorney upon surrender of this Certificate properly endorsed.

IN WITNESS WHEREOF, the said Corporation has caused this Certificate to be signed by its duly authorized officers and its Corporate Seal to be hereunto affixed this 9 day of Nov. A.D. 1935.

Michael Pemlin Goldstein   Secretary   President

$5.00

On February 14, fifty-five men in the employ of the T. Eaton Company, of Toronto, were discharged for refusing to sew with machines the linings in women's coats. They claimed that this change in the method of finishing garments would deprive finishers of their work. On the following day 500 employees of the same Company, 200 of whom were females, were discharged for refusing to work. No settlement was reported at the end of the month.
The Labour Gazette, (April 1912).

What the immigrants in the garment industry feared most was the total destruction of skill categories and an end to the division of jobs based on skills. Ironically it was the needs and the numbers of the immigrants themselves which threatened the artisan structure. A combination of sewing machines, petty entrepreneurship and masses of willing semi-skilled hands meant that employers could break with traditional non-assembly line methods. Strikes for job security or for closed shops were, when it came down to it, strikes against the introduction of a sub-contracting system. Sub-contracting had undercut skilled tradesmen in other fields even before it affected the garment industry. At first the Jewish immigrant community was on both sides of the question. Greenhorns made their way or at least survived by working in little sweatshops in the Ward doing piecework for sub-contractors. Others dreamed of becoming employers themselves. By 1912 though, it was obvious that trade unions could protect everyone, not just the skilled older craftsmen who were often from the British Isles or earlier Jewish immigrant stock. The result was remarkable solidarity among cloakmakers, garment workers, and tailors in the strike against Eaton's in 1912. The solidarity crossed ethnic lines, although the Jewish workers were clearly leaders in the effort.

Union politics were not the only political concern of the Jewish community. Concern for those left behind in the Russian Pale during the First World War was heightened by news of new pogroms carried out by warring armies and bands in the successor states to the Tsarist and Habsburg monarchies. At the same time, the centuries-old dream of an end to the diaspora and a return to Palestine seemed to be taking a step forward with the British Mandate in Palestine and the possibilities of Jewish settlement there. Our pictures suggest a dichotomy in which those concerned with Canadian social politics were young and working class while those who worried most about the fruition of Zionism were older and more middle-class members of the Jewish community. There may be some truth in that, but in fact there were very active Zionist youth groups and among the strike activists in 1912 were many older men and women who had begun their socialist activism as Bundists in the Russian Pale many years before.

Top right: Pickets of the newly organized International Ladies Garment Workers' Union during the Eaton's strike, 1912

Bottom right: Roumanian Jewish women rally in support of the British Mandate in Palestine, 1920

176

Should the immigration of foreigners be encouraged? The crucial question here is the question of the effect of foreign immigration on the character of the electorate.... What will the effect on the country be of a large foreign vote, unfamiliar with the spirit of our institutions and ignorant of our political history? Will they cast their votes intelligently? Or will they sell their franchise for a mess of potage?

W.S. Wallace. "The Canadian Immigration Policy," in *The Canadian Magazine* (February 1908), p.36.

occupations in the customs house or the liquor trade that clearly involved political patronage and some relationship to Ward or machine politics in the city or provincial government. Harry Corti, the editor of an Italian newspaper in the Ward, had some influence, particularly in the war years. He was an active supporter of Elizabeth Neufeld of Central Neighbourhood House and other suffragettes who tried to interest immigrant women in the vote.

Judge Jacob Cohen outside City Hall, 1919

The first to challenge the hold that British and Canadian politicians had on municipal government were the Jews. In one sense this was not immigrant politics; many Jewish families had come to Toronto after an English experience in their migration from Germany or eastern Europe, and many had been in the country as long as German or Irish politicians. On the other hand, since these Jewish leaders showed concern for and received support from many of their more recently arrived co-religionists, their rise to political prominence did reflect power bases that were partly ethnic in character. Louis Singer, who was elected alderman in 1914, fought successfully against an attempt by a xenophobic City Council to disenfranchise all citizens of foreign birth during the war. As early as 1924, Nathan Phillips was an alderman and on the path that would lead him to become the first Jewish mayor of the city. The closest thing to a power broker to emerge in those years was Judge Jacob Cohen. He was made a magistrate by the Ontario government in 1918.

Perhaps because there were few earlier immigrants on the road to assimilation, other groups like the Italians or Macedonians had fewer visible leaders involved in Toronto politics before the First World War. It is noticeable that some second- and third-generation Italians had

Had the women not received the splendid tribute of 26,288 votes we might have said what a farce was a certain scene in the City Hall yesterday morning. First came a long line of Yiddish gentlemen, who seemed to form part of a personally conducted expedition to a certain polling booth. Next came a dozen Chinamen. Then we saw two brilliant varsity girl watchers beseech the Celestials to remember the women. Fine spectacle! Anglo-Saxon women having to ask part of the Chinese Republic to give them votes! Just how valuable educated women may be as municipal workers was revealed when you saw them challenge voters in their own tongues. Frenchmen, Italians, or Spanish, many heard the query, "Will you remember the married women?" in their native tongue.

The Toronto Star (February 1914).

The tone of this account suggests that the press and the public were not accustomed to think of the immigrants as politically sophisticated nor to expect them to vote in blocs. The question of women's suffrage and, even more, the question of wartime government, drew many of the newcomers into political activity and awareness. The city at large viewed with some condescension the immigrant motives for voting and understanding of the political process.

During and after the First World War, the newcomers began to realize their power within in the context of city wards; so, parallel to the growth of trade union activities, there began a process of joining and ultimately controlling local aldermanic machines and then riding associations. In most cases, the various groups, with the exception of the Jews, did not produce their own successful candidates, but they did elect Irish and other older stock politicians who understood their debt to the community and operated successful patronage systems.

Picnic of Ward 4 (Kensington Market area) group of the Liberal-Conservative Association

Annual Picnic
Ward 4 - Liberal Conservative Assn
at Lakeside Park, Port Dalhousie

6 CHANGE AND PERSISTENCE IN IMMIGRANT LIFE

Many young men had come to Toronto in the early 1900s without their families. Often, after years of saving and hard work, they stood waiting expectantly at Union Station for the arrival of loved ones from home. The prepaid steamship tickets had been sent months before; the family's affairs in the village or *shtetl* had been settled, and now the "'crossing,'" the migration process of the family itself, had almost been completed. When they arrived, the newcomers were taken aback by how "Canadian" the one who waited for them appeared and acted; he, in turn, had not expected his wife or nephew or brother to be such a greenhorn. The man who had spent all those years in Toronto or the Ontario north digging ditches or peddling tinwares was still considered a Jew or an Italian by the Anglo-Canadians that he encountered in his daily business; yet he was a Canadian to his newly arrived kinsman.

What were the changes that the newcomer observed in his "Canadian" relative? Were they only subtleties of intonation or accent? Was it simply the Toronto-made suit that he wore? Did new gestures and carriage suggest a new outlook on life? Whatever the differences that separated them were, they reflected the divergence in the paths taken by each person. Life and society in European town or village, particularly in the years around the First World War, had changed radically. Villages that had been Turkish or Russian respectively when men left might be Greek or Polish when their brothers came from them ten years later. On the other hand, no matter how much the early immigrant had tried to cling to old ways, his life style had bent to the exigencies of surviving in Canada. Things that were unself-conscious in the newcomer were awkward and vestigial in the man who had been here ten years.

North American historians have generally assumed a continuum from the decision to migrate taken in the old country to the point several generations later of assimilation into the mainstream of life on this continent. That view is obviously too simple. The photographs in this chapter depict such a kaleidoscope of identities, choices, stages and patterns that one can see immediately that immigrant life cannot be explained by any amount of academic jargon. Men were not absorbed, integrated, acculturated or assimilated. Rather they lived their lives in the new city, and the will to change or persist in their ways interacted with the opportunities that they encountered. Life for the immigrant was a never-ending series of conscious and unconscious adaptations of old ways to new situations. No individual family, or immigrant group went through the process in exactly the same manner. Where one man refused to speak English with his children at the dinner table, another delighted in their street slang, the use of which was a sign to him that his children were "making it" in the city. Some parents had come to North America to free themselves from the social and religious constraints of village life, while others devoted their energies toward re-creating village life here, shepherding their children to every religious, seasonal, or folkloric occasion of their people. In other words, the immigrant world was as varied as its components, brave men who had made free choices. When one ponders that fact, social scientific concepts like generation and assimilation appear more and more inadequate. Brothers from the same town in Italy went their separate ways, one to the Methodist mission, the other to Our Lady of Mt. Carmel. The children of the former returned to Catholicism in the second generation; the children of the latter fell into agnosticism. In neither case was generational or religious conflict in the family significantly different from that of Irish, English or Scots around them.

Yet the immigrants *were* distinct from the large city around them. They lived in sections of the city that were not quite "Canadian"; yet those neighbourhoods were not culturally or socially the same as the village or town left behind in Europe. Such neighbourhoods existed as a response to the prejudice of the receiving society, but they were also a spontaneous result of the common culture and the common economic plight of the immigrants. So, in several senses, the newcomer had not finished his migration when he reached Toronto. The psychic and physical trip from his Old World setting to his full acceptance of the consequences of his decision to migrate and to his full acceptance by Canadian society lay ahead of him. If we realize that the state of being immigrant did not end at some artificial line drawn on a pier in Halifax or at Ellis Island, then we can see that the in-migration process went on for some time after people arrived. The crossing did not end in the Ward or Kensington Market any more than it had at the port of disembarkation. Some travelled on from the landlocked steerage of the immigrant neighbourhood within one generation; some ended their trip there. Others returned to end their days in the Old World villages from which they had migrated; yet others anglicized their names and passed completely from the records of the immigrant community.

It is easy enough to make generalizations about immigrant neighbourhoods. For example, the survival of Jewish or Italian group life in the Ward depended on the size and vitality of the group and conversely on the barriers of prejudice that each group faced. We can measure the presence of Jewish or Italian life in the area by counting storefronts, clubs, and churches or synagogues that served the immigrants. But how would we measure the "immigrant-ness"—the ethnicity, to use the social scientific jargon — of the individual or his family. Surely, we could not depend on anything so mechanical as family name. Nothing is revealed about a man by his Italian, Jewish, Macedonian or other surname. For example, the first well-known "Italian" in the city of Toronto, Captain Philip De Grassi, had been a British officer in the West Indies and had taught languages in Chichester, England, for fifteen years before he arrived in Toronto. Since the census of 1921 shows most of the prewar immigrants to Toronto learning English, language use will not provide a key to those who dwell between the Old World and Canadian society. Perhaps prejudice and discrimination from older Torontonians would be our best guide to who remained a foreigner in the city.

There is, then, no honest "checklist of ethnicity" that can be applied to individual newcomers. The same activities or occasions that reinforced one man's commitment to his primary national group tied another to a larger Canadian society. Entertainment, sports, weddings — there were foreign varieties of each in the city in the 1920s, but their connotation and impact was clear only to those who saw them with xenophobic eyes. For example, the Irish priest who saw Italian Catholic weddings as barbarous foreign ritual missed the point that the marriage ended the migrant ways of a navvy and committed him to a Canadian life and Canadian children. The opening of Yiddish theatres may have provided cultural persistence for Jews from larger cities of the Pale and from Odessa; it also moved into a uniquely North American relationship with the development of vaudeville talent and of impresarios. Playing soccer with co-nationals guarded some from the North American environment, but the very moves of soccer were parallelled in ice hockey, and Canadian conditions and expectations caused migration from pitch to rink.

In a previous chapter, the ways in which the children were weaned from their parents by the schools were discussed. Nowhere could the gap in values between the immigrant father and the Canadian authorities be greater than the question of sport. Toronto educators, imbued with British imperial values, saw sport and clean athletic competition at the very heart of the civilization that they wished to maintain. While sports provided a rehearsal for leadership roles in society among well-born children, for the poor and the immigrant, athletics could teach many of the lessons about the "Canadian way": fair play, team effort, and of course, healthy bodies as the temples of the Almighty. Neither the Jewish merchant from the small towns of Poland and Russia nor the Christian villager could comprehend all that. Italian men played bocce (a variety of lawn bowls); older men of other nationalities played cards for relaxation but to run about a football field or soccer pitch in the rain and snow or to lose teeth to a hockey stick seemed both wasteful and insane. Some later immigrants who came from middle-class or urban areas supported soccer clubs as an extension of their national identity, but on the continent, at least, soccer had not yet become the classless and universal pastime that emerged later. Traditional activities like gymnastics, wrestling and fencing survived among Slavs and Finns.

Three sports drew parent and child together; prize fighting was a downtown, often immigrant, game and the chance to make one's way in America with one's fists tempted many young men. Basketball, because it was a game of settlement houses, small schoolyards, and YMCA's had some appeal. The equipment was cheap and, as with boxing, there were immigrant stars to emulate. Without doubt, though, the game that was quintessentially North American was baseball. The immigrant parents and children shared big league heroes; the schools organized baseball teams from the earliest grades on. The game offered skills without violence and a cheap way to idle away summer twilights. At least one immigrant's son from the sandlots of Toronto made the Big League, playing for the Brooklyn Dodgers. Teams represented more than neighbourhoods. There were Macedonian, Jewish and Italian teams. At the same time, on little downtown diamonds or at Christie Pits, sharp-eyed scouts watched the way a boy threw or hit before they noticed his "ethnic" background. As with so many aspects of life in North America, the world of sports had no real equivalent in the rural and small-town areas of the old country.

The immigrants and the children of immigrants lived between the ways of where they had come from and the ways of Canada. The photographs in this chapter suggest that the persistence of some Old World habits and the loss of others differed enormously from family to family and from group to group. What is even truer is that we cannot measure—pictures or not—the intensity of meaning behind seemingly small things. An Armenian family picnic may have been as total and intense an experience, as much a link with a lost homeland, as a more elaborate gala such as the annual meeting of a national society. Peasant dialect spoken quickly to a parent, in love or anger, may have had more resilience and meaning than elaborate religious or language schools on Saturdays. Endogamy, marrying in one's own immigrant group, may not have survived because of careful chaperoning and church dances but rather because of fear of people of other groups. Did intermarriage come with the passing of fear and prejudice?

Despite the prejudice and poverty around them, the newcomers inherently knew the value of the struggle for pluralism and democracy against elitism and demands for conformity. For them Canadian freedom simply meant the right to define their own existence and to retain what they wished of one world while taking their place in a new one.

186

The Ukrainian is a race purely Slav, gay, chivalrous, made thoughtful by its own steppes — a race of poets, musicians, artists who have fixed for all time their national history in the songs of the people which no centuries of oppression could silence. The singers — the Kobzars — accompany themselves on the kobza while they sing the glories of the Ukraine. All art with them is national, from the building of their tiny huts to the embroideries which adorn their clothes and which are distinguished for their originality all over the east.

J.W. Gibbon, ''The Foreign Born'' (June 1920), p.337.

Although the prairies were the heartland of Ukrainian settlement in Canada, Toronto rapidly became a centre of Ukrainian culture as well. The Rev. Kolesnikoff reported to the Baptist mission board before the First World War that there were over 400 Ruthenians in the Ward. With the defeat of the Ukrainian National Republic, more Ukrainians came to Toronto in the 1920s. The struggle to keep alive a separate national tradition had depended in eastern Europe on an alliance between Ukrainian intellectuals and poets and the folklore of the common people. That alliance was reforged in North America. Every folkloric expression of the Ukrainians served also to reinforce the principles of national survival in the face of first Tsarist Russian imperialism and then of the Bolshevik threat to a culture based on small farms and small villages.

Choral groups, operas, and folk dance troupes were formed that involved large numbers of the immigrant community and provided a framework in which the children of the immigrants could be educated to the dreams and ways of their parents and their grandparents. Although differences existed between Orthodox and Catholic in the Ukrainian community, very few people wished to give up their culture for the ways of a Canadian city.

Ukrainian folk and dance groups, c. 1925

There are nine synagogues in Toronto. One of them was for sixteen years a large Methodist church —built during the famous "boom" of 1888. A people with nine churches, a Cosmopolitan Club, and twenty thousand population were surely entitled to a drama of their own; to plays given in Yiddish, the language of the ancient Bible.

Augustus Bridle, "The Drama of the 'Ward'" in *The Canadian Magazine* (November 1909), p.3.

The old Agnes Street Methodist Church was converted into the Lyric Theatre in 1909. Travelling companies from the Yiddish theatres of New York were brought to the city by impresarios. Over the front door of the former church, a large marquee with signs in Yiddish and English was erected. The interior of the structure was completely reconstructed, but the old Methodist pews were kept as gallery seats. Seating over a thousand people, the Lyric offered gallery tickets for twenty-five cents and seats in the orchestra for seventy-five. Other Yiddish theatres came later. While no other immigrant group had an extensive or commercial theatre life, the vaudeville tradition and then the cheap movie houses had a very large immigrant clientele. In fact, the English and the mores learned at Saturday matinees probably had as much to do with acculturation as did any amount of formal schooling.

Some members of the Italian community pooled their funds and sent one youngster to wait for the box office to open when visiting musical maestri like Caruso passed through Toronto on tour. Every immigrant group in the city sought through folkloric, choral, or amateur dramatic associations to retain their ancestral culture and to impart it to their Canadian-born offspring. Since many immigrants came from unlettered backgrounds, retention of folksongs and dances was more common than mainte-

nance of a "higher" literary culture. Yet a remarkable number of men and women could quote Dante or Shevchenko at length or recite parts of some national poem like *The Kalevala.* Their children grew up assuming that the little snatches of lullabies and wise old sayings that they heard in childhood were peculiar to their family culture. It was often an unsettling experience later in life to find those same tunes and axioms in a Puccini opera or a Chekhov play. Only then did one sense the amount of culture and wistfulness that immigrant parents displayed.

Right: Strand Theatre, Spadina and Dundas, originally built to be a Yiddish theatre, 1930

Below: Lyric Theatre

The human soul is thirsty for joy and happiness, and these feelings are stronger when one lives in torment. The struggle for life did not hinder their wish for recreation. On the contrary, it made them want to meet each other to celebrate together, and to get the feeling that they were in the Old Country. They celebrated all the church holidays, incorporated them with their traditions. They celebrated namedays. They sang patriotic and folk songs. They danced 'horos' (a chain dance). They talked about their places of birth, about their families and relatives, about the heroic 'chetnicks' (freedom fighters) and their leaders, and for the struggles of their people. In short, they spoke about everything connected with their lives in their homeland.

Foto Tomev, *Short History of Zhelevo Village Macedonia* (Zhelevo Brotherhood of Toronto, 1971), pp 77-78.

Benevolent societies and village brotherhoods had begun as efforts to protect the immigrant worker from sudden hardship or to pay burial costs. As conditions improved and incomes rose, such associations naturally assumed a role as centres of immigrant culture. Even though they were remote from events in Europe, many immigrants passed from local village loyalties to nationalism in the years around the First World War. For most of the immigrant cultures and for most of the nationalist movements back in the successor states of the Habsburg, Romanov and Ottoman empires, the glorification of folkways and the assertion of peasant democracy served as a bridge of understanding. A dance, a song or a costume went from being a simple ethnic reality to being a defiant or triumphal proof of nationalist culture. The same men who founded the first Serbian society in the city were the proudest members of the new Yugoslav-Canadian Association.

Well before there was a free Finland, the Finns in North America had comprehensive national and social institutions. Socialist federations and even temperance societies nurtured a national culture and a nationality in exile. Indeed, when one looks at the Vapaus (Freedom) organizations in Sudbury and Toronto, they seem to meet all the needs of the immigrant, with mutual aid societies, bookstores, a newspaper, steamship agency and labour bureau and support for cultural and choral groups all combined. Yet a scant few years before the war, the only official protection for the Finn in North America was the Tsarist consulate. One can see why the immigrants were often an important part of the new nation-states in Europe. Various *doms* (national houses) among the western and southern Slavic immigrants in the city served as cultural centres for their people in the same manner as the Vapaus did for the Finns.

Bottom: Vapaus Finnish bookstore

Top: Yugoslav-Canadian Association at St. Paul's Hall on King Street, 1930

For this you must begin as boys, to look on all classes of boys as your friends. Remember, whether rich or poor, from town or country, you are all Britons in the first place, and you've got to continue to make Britain a power for good in the world.

Lord Baden-Powell, *Scouting for Boys*, Special Canadian Edition, n.d., p.280.

The word Briton, one assumes, could have been a very useful device in an imperial world that was truly a melting pot. Although the word is redolent of Kipling and racist doggerel, there was ambivalence between a White Anglo-Saxon concept of hegemony and a belief that a new man, inspired by free institutions and the British way, was being forged from many nationalities. A Briton, much like an ancient Roman, could come from anywhere in the Empire. As the boy scout manual put it, "almost every race, every kind of man black, white or yellow, in the world furnishes subjects of King George V." Young men could be made to behave in the manner of a mythical Briton: that was the "civilizing mission" in colonies where the majority were non-white, but it was also the "acculturating mission" in colonies like Canada where the free economic flow of immigration threatened to create a polyglot society that might not understand the Empire and its needs. The Boy Scouts, like so many of the organizations in the New World, encouraged some cultural pluralism but had as its ideal the creation of a homogeneous man. It was not a process of deliberate cultural genocide. The civilizers assumed the superiority of British culture and therefore also assumed that the well-being of their young wards depended upon the degree to which they could join that higher civilization. The child of immigrant parents in Toronto might find that his scoutmaster tried to make him a Briton; his schoolteacher tried to Canadianize him; his

parents insisted on Old World values and loyalties, and the Saturday matinees and pop culture around him tied him ineluctably to the style and values of the United States.

Chinese boy scout troop in High Park, 1919

196

Athletic competition and sport groups did not invariably draw people into the melting pot. Certain things like gymnastics, the *sokol* of the Czechs and the *turnverein* of the Germans, were as central to cultural retention as any folk dance or literature. Fencing, Graeco-Roman wrestling and long-distance running were also culturally important to some of the immigrant groups.

Soccer, of course, did not have the universality that it was to develop. It tended to be the game of the British Isles immigrants. Professional soccer leagues had not emerged in most of the European countries and few people from rural area had had an opportunity to develop interest or skill in the sport. Competitive bicycle racing attracted much attention in the immigrant press. National clubs and associations, as they became involved with the urban culture of the home countries, did begin to field soccer teams. The degree to which sports led to assimilation or cultural retention was not clearly related to the sport played. As much national feeling went into fielding a Macedonian hockey team as into the more traditional Balkanski Unak. Young Tommy Ivan, who went on to fame in the National Hockey League, participated in both activities.

Finnish wrestlers

Top right: Czechoslovak soccer team, 1929

Bottom right: Italian gymnasts

PRVY ČESKOSLOVENSKÝ FODBALOVÝ CLOB ZALOŽENÝ
v CANADE TORONTO 1929

198

118 lbs — M. Kosloff v. G. Moscow. This bout was very well contested and had the crowd on their toes all the way through, but Kid Kosloff by his ring generalship managed to beat his opponent by a slight margin. . . . The best all around performer in this line was L. Mandel. He was closely followed by W. Gold, who although only a midget in size, certainly showed how the fish game ought to be played. He also gave an exhibition of fancy swimming and diving.

Central Neighbourhood House, Newspaper Clipping Collection Scrapbook.

Baseball and basketball were the games of the public schools, the playgrounds, and the settlement houses. Boxing, while it went on at the YMCA and elsewhere, lived in a twilight between the practice of manliness and the hint of corruption in downtown gyms and clubs. Jewish parents had to make a transition from seeing the kid on the sandlot as a good-for-nothing who should have been helping his father in the shop or practising on his violin to acknowledging the importance of sports to their children.

In those days before the shrinking of city space and the decline of the elaborate minor league system in baseball, a youngster could play baseball from his first walking years until he was middle-aged. Along the way, there were tryouts with semi-pro and pro teams and the complete absence of ethnic barriers in a world where only performance really mattered.

Above: Baseball at St. Christopher's House

Right: City Park Senior Basketball Championship, "Judeans" *versus* "Ostler," 1915

Overleaf left: McCaul Street Public School basketball team, 1912

Overleaf right: Hockey at Central Neighbourhood House

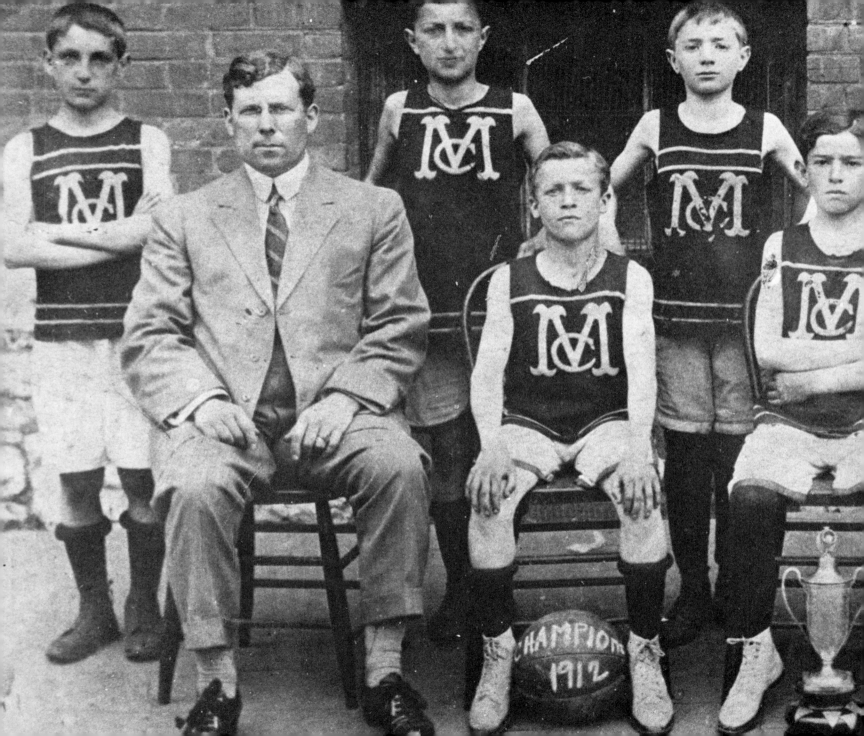

Rev. Michael J. Biro, Buffalo
Rev and Dear Father,
        I am requested by His Grace
Archbishop McEvay to acknowledge the re-
ceipt of your letter re Marriage of Hungarians.
His Grace grants you the faculty of uniting in
Marriage all the Hungarians of this Diocese who do
not speak any other language but their own, and
who bring to you a letter from their Pastor. Also they
must be married in Buffalo as you have not the
permission according to the Civil Law to perform the
Ceremony in Canada.
                Yours sincerely in Christ,
                John J. Kidd Secretary.
                Toronto   Dec. 10, 1908

Archdiocese of Toronto Archives

The word "immigration" lacks precision. Does
it mean that a man has ended his journey when he passes a
border point or survives a battery of medical officers and
immigration officials? When, in fact, has one come into a
new society and settled? For many the sensation of being
in motion went on even after they reached Toronto. For
the early migrant bachelors, immigration as the passing of
state boundaries or arriving in port or city meant practically nothing. The sign that a man had finished his psychic
trek often came when he sent back to his village or town
society to find a suitable bride, or when he married another
newcomer in North America. In a sense, weddings, births,
and deaths celebrated the arrival and permanent settlement in North America. Usually weddings were community events affecting immigrants and small towns in
Europe alike.
        To the degree that the service resembled that of
the old country, to the extent that the witnesses and guests
were countrymen, and, of course, as long as the marriage
partners came from the same town or region in Europe, the
wedding in Toronto was not just the creation of a new
nuclear family or the proof of the permanence of immigration; it was above all a proof of the well-being and sustain-
ing power of the immigrant colony. Husband, wife and
their future children had been welcomed and bound into
the fate of a group that was neither identical with the old
country or completely Canadian. A collectivity of families
with links to each other and to the ways of a common old
country may be the most uncomplicated and truthful origin of the concept of ethnic groups in North America. It
was certainly a powerful incentive to democratic pluralism.

Right: Polish wedding group

Below: Macedonian wedding group

204

When it came to an urgent matter such as a funeral it helped even non-members as long as they were Zhelevtsi. The brotherhood helped the family of the deceased priest Elia Atanasov Trayanov in Bulgaria by sending his family $300.00.

F. Tomev, *Short History of Zhelevo Village Macedonia*, p.95.

The deceased in our picture did not have to depend on his friends or his *società di muto soccorso* to provide him with a funeral that matched the ritual of his Old World home. In life he had been a successful pasta manufacturer in Toronto, and his funeral reflected his North American accomplishments and his loyalty to Italian ways. Very few newcomers or their kinsmen were willing to compromise with urban Canadian mores when it came to the final rite of passage. The thought of death is discomfitting to all men, but in the stable rural and religious societies from which the migrants came, death had a more rhythmic and natural place in collective community life than it did in the North American city. The small comfort of knowing that one would be interred beside loved ones in sight of fields and places that had been part of family existence for centuries was denied to those who dared to emigrate, and it disturbed them greatly. Even the most determined immigrant in his dreams of New World opportunity for himself or his children had trouble thinking of the finality of separation from his culture and origins that would come if he died without benefit of his clergy and countrymen in America. Galician emigrants carried a handful of native soil in a handkerchief across the sea to Canada. That soil was reverently thrown into their North American graves.

The Jews, minorities even in their lands of origin, had always formed close-knit burial societies. In Toronto, Chevra Kadisha, the burial society, served also as way of bringing together men from the same Russian ghetto or *shtetl* and to constantly renew local loyalties and reassure one another that there was a human scale to life and death in the large and foreign city of Toronto. Before they were able to create national parishes and find sympathetic clergy, Italian, Polish and Lithuanian brotherhoods and benevolent societies, also often based on common origin in small European communities, looked after their own dead.

Funeral of an Italian pasta manufacturer and businessman, 1922

We have absorbed, perfectly I think, the thousand Italians and some three thousand Jews who were in Toronto according to the Census of 1891.

P.H. Bryce, "Civic Responsibility and the Increase of Immigration," Empire Club of Canada. *Addresses*, 1906–07 (Toronto 1907), p.189.

In some ways both cultural persistence and assimilation were in the eyes of the beholder. An old man drinks his unsweetened wine from a used coca cola bottle under the arbour in his backyard. If a social worker looked over the fence in the laneway, she saw an immigrant with a bad and "foreign" drinking habit. If a fellow Macedonian happened by, the two men would share their melancholy, talk of the inferior Canadian grapes, inferior soil, and the heroic exploits of their ancestors. In fact, there is no way to measure the intensity of feeling that surrounded the acts of immigrating and settling. Except for superficialities of style and accent, degrees of assimilation, acculturation, absorption varied in the different parts of a man's existence. A man who insisted that his grandchildren call him *nono* or *zeydeh* had endured many years when his own children called him dad or pa. When visitors came from the old country, he had been ashamed to discover that he no longer spoke his own language adequately. He cared passionately about the well-being of his children and his kind in Toronto and Canada and so he had powerful reasons to care about Canada. He accepted hardship and prejudice as the consequence of his rash act of migration but assumed that prosperity for his children was also a consequence of that act. If he received respect from his children and their children, it proved that his act of migration had made good sense and yet at the same time, it provided a sense of ageless continuity of family that had been so much a part of life in the old country.

210

The presence in Canada of many people whose language and culture are distinctive by reason of their birth or ancestry represents an inestimable enrichment that Canadians cannot afford to lose. The dominant cultures can only profit from the influence of these other cultures. Linguistic variety is unquestionably an advantage, and its beneficial effects on the country are priceless. We have constantly declared our desire to see all Canadians associating in a climate of equality, whether they belong to the Francophone or Anglophone society. Members of "other ethnic groups," which we prefer to call cultural groups, must enjoy these same advantages and meet the same restrictions. Integration, with respect for both the spirit of democracy and the most deep-rooted human values, can engender healthy diversity within a harmonious and dynamic whole.

The Cultural Contribution of the Other Ethnic Groups, Volume IV of the Report of the Royal Commission on Bilingualism and Biculturalism, p.14.

Yacob Yoseph Goldenberg and his grandson, Henoch

Photograph Credits

Baptist Women's Missionary Society of Ontario and Quebec, Baptist
    Archives: 63, 134, left; 153; 154; 155.
Alfreda Baradziej Family Collection: 203.
Bernardo Family Collection: 99
Bureau of Municipal Research: 30.
Canadian Jewish Congress, Central Region Archives: 103, 173, top; 209
    left.
Canadian Pacific: 21.
Central Neighbourhood House: 43, top; 44; 126; 127; 130; 134, right; 135;
    156; 201.
Constantine Stephen Chreston Collection: 85
Ann Durjancik Family Collection: 197, top.
Eatons of Canada Archives: 76, 77; 78.
Joseph Eisenberg Collection: 179
William Eisenberg Family Collection: 81; 168
Mrs. B. Goldman Family Collection: 9
Helen & Henry Goldenberg Family Collection: 19, left; 88; 208, right;
    211.
Esther (Walerstein) Grant Collection: 93; 173, bottom.
Hospital for Sick Children, Archives: 140, 141; 143.
International Ladies Garment Workers Union, Toronto: 175, top.
James Collection of Early Canadiana: 83; 89; 91, left; 102, left; 106; 157;
    175, bottom.
Martha Kujanpaa Family Collection: 91, right; 196.

Library of Congress: 13.
50th. Anniversary Jubilee Almanac of the Macedono-Bulgarian
    Orthodox Cathedral, Toronto, 1960: 160.
B. M. Markovich Family Collection: 92; 170; 193, above; 207, left
Metropolitan Toronto Library Board: 82; 101; 121; 205.
Archives of Ontario: 17, 29; 40; 90.
George Petroff Family Collection: 8; 10; 12; 18; 95; 169; 202; 206; 207,
    bottom right
Public Archives of Canada: 39; 43, bottom; 47; 49; 61; 86; 104; 105; 159;
    167; 195.
Morris Roitman Family Collection: 11.
E. Tarvainen Family Collection: 123; 193, below.
Tatarian Family Collection, 208, top left; 209, top right.
Theodore Family Collection: 59; 208, bottom left.
Foto S. Tomev Collection: 161
City of Toronto Archives: 31; 32; 33; 34; 35; 37; 45; 48; 62; 65; 66; 67; 68;
    69; 70; 71; 72; 73; 74; 80; 84; 102, right; 107; 115; 119; 133; 136; 137;
    139; 166; 177; 191; 199.
Toronto Borad of Education: 165.
Toronto Playground Association, courtesy of Harriet Parsons; 128; 129.
Toronto Transit Commission: 75; 122.
Turner-Egier Family Collection: 200.
Ukrainian National Home, Toronto: 187; 188; 189.
United Church Archives: ii; 14; 15; 20; 19, right; 41; 42; 46; 79; 87; 94;
    97; 98; 117; 125; 131; 142; 162; 163; 190; 197, bottom; 198; 207, top
    right; 209, bottom right; title page.
Zlote Poklosie, Toronto, 1961: 171.